OUT OF
CURIOSITY

Restoring the Power of Hungry
Minds for Better Schools,
Workplaces, and Lives

McREL
INTERNATIONAL
Denver, Colorado USA

Bryan GOODWIN

McREL International

4601 DTC Boulevard, Suite 500

Denver, CO 80237 USA

Phone: 303.337.0990 | Fax: 303.337.3005

Website: www.mcrel.org | Email: info@mcrel.org | Store: store.mcrel.org

---

About McREL

McREL International helps educators flourish by turning research into solutions that transform teaching, learning, and leading.

McREL is a nonprofit, nonpartisan education research and development organization that since 1966 has turned knowledge about what works in education into practical, effective guidance and training for teachers and education leaders across the U.S. and around the world.

All referenced trademarks are the property of the respective owners. All internet links mentioned in this book are correct as of the initial publication date.

Printed in the United States of America.

To order, visit store.mcrel.org.

ISBN: 978-0-9993549-6-4

Library of Congress Control Number: 2018908626

Goodwin, B. (2018). *Out of curiosity: Restoring the power of hungry minds for better schools, workplaces, and lives.* Denver, CO: McREL International.

OUT OF CURIOSITY

Restoring the Power of Hungry Minds for Better Schools, Workplaces, and Lives

To my lovely daughters, Sophie, Emma, and Molly; stay curious.
And to my wife, Kristi; thanks for being my partner
in chasing horizons.

Acknowledgements

A book like this is never a solo effort. I wish to thank Ron Miletta, Roger Fiedler, and Eric Hübler for being my thought partners and helping to shape and reshape this book into its present form. I must also thank the production team of Roger, Eric, Christine H. Schmidt, and Judy Counley for their keen editorial eyes, wizardry with words, and artistic creativity seen throughout the wonderful design and layout of this book. Deep thanks to Fred Ende, Pete Hall, Kim Marshall, Harvey Silver, and Randy Ziegenfuss for their early reviews and encouragement, as well as the thousands of educators, researchers, and business leaders I've encountered in the two decades since I joined McREL; they've all inspired me, and I hope I've returned the favor at least a few times. Finally, I owe a tremendous debt of gratitude to Wayne Craig, who first piqued my own curiosity about the topic of curiosity. Thanks to you all for making this book become a reality.

A Cure for What Ails Us

" The human brain had a vast memory storage.
It made us curious and very creative. Those were
the characteristics that gave us an advantage—
curiosity, creativity and memory. "

– David Suzuki

Cheating Death

In the mid-1980s, Gary Swan and Dorit Carmelli,[1] researchers at SRI International, rounded up more than 1,000 men who had participated in a three-decade study of their health behaviors and outcomes to ask them an unusual set of questions. By now, the men were all around 70 years old with plenty known about their medical histories: blood pressure and cholesterol levels, frequency of drinking and smoking, whether they had fought cancer or heart disease, education levels, cognitive abilities, and general mental health. Following a hunch that a subtle yet powerful dimension of personality could be a critical, hidden driver of their health outcomes, Swan and Carmelli asked the men and, for good measure, their wives, to respond a 10-question survey . . . and then sat patiently on the answers for five years.

When they reconnected with the couples in 1991, they found that among the 2,000-plus people originally surveyed, 126 men and 78 women had passed away. That simple fact created a comparison group of survivors and non-survivors and invited a captivating question: Was there anything in the men's medical histories (no similar medical histories were available for the women) or in how they had answered those 10 simple questions five years earlier that might have predicted their shorter lifespans?

As it turns out, the answer was yes. How both men and women answered those questions revealed a subtle, yet powerful, facet of their personalities, which in turn appeared to predict their longevity.

The survivors demonstrated higher levels of a single, key *personality* trait than those who had died. In fact, for the men, only age and cancer seemed to be more predictive of their mortality. In other words, a personality trait seemed to be more strongly tied to their mortality than their cholesterol levels, smoking, education levels, and mental health. For both men and women, in fact, scoring one standard deviation above the mean (or at the 84th percentile) on the survey reduced their risk of dying five years later by about 30 percent.

So, what was it? What personality trait helped these study participants live longer?

You'll find the answer on the following page.

Well done. You turned the page.

In a way, that simple action reflects what the survivors in Swan and Carmelli's study were more capable of doing than non-survivors—demonstrating *curiosity*. The short personality test had asked the senior citizens to rate themselves on a scale of 1 to 4 on statements like these: "I feel like exploring my environment," "I feel stimulated," and "I feel eager."

At first, Swan and Carmelli were at a bit of a loss to explain exactly *why* such a strong link between curiosity and longevity would exist. One possibility, they surmised, might be that fading levels of curiosity are a canary in the coal mine, warning of the onset of Alzheimer's or other deterioration in the brain. Yet another possibility was that as people age, they often face health and mobility challenges, so curiosity might predict whether they approach such challenges as solvable problems, or succumb to despair and decreased interpersonal interactions, hastening their demise. All Swan and Carmelli could say for sure was that more curious seniors were more likely to be alive five years later.

Confronting our contradictions about curiosity

Despite this and many other powerful benefits of curiosity, we humans tend to have mixed views about it, as individuals and as a society. Consider all the stories and inherited wisdom we've absorbed since our youth that paint curiosity as lurid fascination and temptation. In the Bible and Greek mythology, curiosity prompts Eve and Pandora, respectively, to unleash evil upon the world. Folk wisdom warns us about "curiosity killing the cat." And not so long ago, Eleanor Roosevelt found herself forced to defend her intellectual curiosity, which her critics groused was unbecoming of a First Lady. Even modern internet searchers seem to harbor caution about curiosity: type the words "is curiosity" into Google's search engine and it auto-fills with the words "a sin."

Certainly, at times, our need for intellectual closure and getting to the bottom of something, even if it means extracting lurid details, *can* reflect morbid curiosity, as researchers discovered when they sat students down at a table and told them to be careful with a pile of ballpoint pens left over from a previous experiment because some were electrified and would shock them if touched. As it turns out, like Pandora peering into her infamous box, the students couldn't resist the "shock value" (pun intended) of touching the pens. [2] Thus, this little experiment appeared to demonstrate that curiosity may sometimes lead us to indulge in counterproductive or self-destructive urges.

Could curiosity be a cure for what ails us?

Nonetheless, as you'll discover in the chapters ahead, curiosity takes many forms. In its various incarnations, it has been shown to have far more positive consequences than negative ones, including:

◊ **Priming the pump for learning.** The *more curious* we are, the more we learn and recall later about our learning. Moreover, curiosity is more strongly linked to student success than IQ; however, the longer students stay in school, they less curious they become.

◊ **Creating better leaders and more engaged workplaces**. With 70 percent of employees disengaged at work, employers should pay attention to this fact: Employee curiosity and engagement are strongly linked. So are the curiosity of executives and their effectiveness as leaders, and the presence of curiosity in companies and their business success.

◊ **Supporting better relationships**. When we're curious about others, we develop stronger relationships with them. However, *interpersonal curiosity* appears to be in short supply, given the worrisome decline in college students' reported levels of empathy since the 1960s and especially steep drop since 2000.

◊ **Making our lives more fulfilling.** On days when we feel curious, we also experience greater personal satisfaction; in short, people who report greater curiosity also report greater levels of happiness and life fulfillment.

What may be most enticing about curiosity is that it's not something we must learn or a skill to be developed. Rather, we're born curious. Yes, some people are more naturally curious than others. Yet as we'll see in this book, curiosity is hardwired in all of us. No one needs to teach us how to be curious.

That's the good news.

Here's the bad news.

As we'll also see throughout this book, childlike curiosity often wanes as we grow older. As any parent knows, toddlers ask lots of questions, almost incessantly. Yet research shows that by the time kids reach school age, their questions come fewer and farther between; whereas toddlers ask up to 100 questions per day, middle schoolers' daily questions dwindle to nearly nil.[3] In short, it appears that as we grow older, we seem to run *out of curiosity*.

Come back, curiosity . . .

Why should that be? Why should something as essential to who we are as human beings start to fade when we become adults? Could it be that we simply acquire more information about our environment and thus have fewer questions about it? Could it be that something in our environment tells us to stop asking so many questions and get on with the business of life? Or could it be that we put ourselves on a need-to-know basis, accepting the world around us as is and no longer experiencing the joy of discovery? To answer these questions, we'll look more deeply at what happens to kids' curiosity when they enter the place that, ostensibly at least, ought to be designed to unleash it: school. We'll also examine what happens to us as adults when we're curious—and when we're not.

Knowing that curiosity leads to better learning, better workplaces, and better lives might lead us to ask a larger question: What would it look like to unleash the deep kind of curiosity that lies at the heart of discovery, science, and enlightenment, and serves as the lifeblood of democracy—across an entire society? That is, what would it look like if we were to arrange more of our schools, our daily lives, our interactions with one another, and our workplaces to do more things *out of curiosity?*

The purpose of this book is to focus our attention on the many (and often subtle) ways in which we seem to quash and run out of curiosity, and what that means for our kids, places of work, society, and happiness. More important, though, we'll explore together how we can restore curiosity in everything we do, making our schools and companies better, leading more fulfilling lives, and creating a better society for us and our children.

Let's get curious

While this book will offer some practical ways to instill curiosity in our classrooms, relationships, and organizations, it's not designed to be a how-to guide or step-by-step manual for being curious (*Curiosity for Dummies*, if you will). Such a book would be counter-productive, because, as we'll see, curiosity doesn't always serve an obvious purpose. Nor does it follow a straight line. Indeed, it's often only when we allow ourselves to engage in some childlike wonder and to engage in a bit of intellectual wandering that we arrive at deeper meaning, richer learning, and greater success.

Thus, this book is intended to pique *your* curiosity and provide you with a deeper appreciation for how so many aspects of our lives and society are better when curiosity is present.

So, if you're curious, let's start wondering and wandering.

Getting Curious About Curiosity

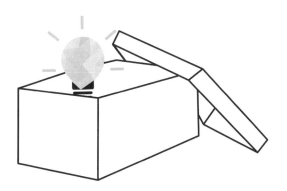

CHAPTER ONE

What Is This Funny Little Thing Called Curiosity?

"Why is the grass green?"

"How come we can see the moon in the day?"

"Where did the dinosaurs go?"

Anyone who's been around a young child for very long knows the barrage of questions they ask, from the mundane ("What's the difference between a burrito and an enchilada?") to the profound ("Why do people die?") to the uncomfortable ("Where do babies come from?").

Sometimes their questions challenge us, testing the limits of our own knowledge.

Shortly before bedtime one evening a few years ago, my daughter, Molly, who was seven at the time, suddenly became engrossed in the inner workings of the fluorescent light bulbs in her ceiling lamp. "Why are the curlicue lights better?" she asked.

I suspected her question was a bedtime-stalling tactic, but felt compelled to answer. "They use less electricity," I said.

However, my answer didn't satisfy her curiosity; she wanted to know *why* they use less electricity.

"They're not as hot, so they turn more electricity into light," I replied.

Still, she was curious: "*Why* don't they get as hot?"

Given that I was fast approaching the limits of my knowledge of interior illumination, I offered a vague explanation about lighting a gas instead of a filament, punctuated with a quip about it being time to turn off the lights and go to sleep.

The spontaneity and doggedness of her questions, though, made *me* curious. Where had her curiosity come from? After all, I'd done nothing to encourage it; her questions had emerged from the inner workings of her mind. And apart from achieving a delay in bedtime of a few seconds, her inquisitiveness didn't serve any purpose beyond the desire to learn *for the sake of learning*. In that regard, her curiosity seemed almost, well, sublime—a reflection of what truly makes us human—an innate desire to seek knowledge, truth, and meaning.

But I'm getting ahead of myself.

A strange phenomenon

One of the first things we might wonder about curiosity is, simply, what the heck is it? And what causes it? We've all experienced the weirdness of curiosity—how it flashes in our minds like a bolt out of the blue, a sudden flash or seemingly invisible hand tugging on our intellect and piquing our imagination.

At times, curiosity can be an irrational drive—a quest for information with little or no material benefit. Consider, for example, supermarket tabloids grabbing our interest in the lives of Hollywood stars. Even more strangely, perhaps, while this sort of curiosity can be a powerful impulse, it's often ephemeral; once through the checkout aisle, we rarely give another thought to those tabloid headlines.

For some, curiosity can manifest itself as a sort of thrill-seeking impulse. We become curious, for example, about skydiving, riding a motorcycle, or jumping off a cliff into the ocean. Or maybe we're drawn to milder (and less risky) thrills, like learning to salsa dance, talking to a new neighbor at a party, or visiting Bhutan. Sometimes we act on those impulses and sometimes we don't. Soon thereafter, the impulse often fades.

At the same time, we've all probably experienced another kind of less fleeting and more intellectual curiosity, something that drives us to keep searching for an answer, following one link after another on the internet or filling our personal library with books on a topic that holds our fascination. In these cases, an initial spark of interest—often, we may even forget when or where it began—becomes a lifelong intellectual pursuit. This brand of deeper, more profound curiosity often lies at the heart of invention, science, and entrepreneurship—think of Thomas Edison and his colleagues experimenting with hundreds of different metals before finally identifying tungsten as the best material for light bulb filaments, or Jane Goodall spending months in the rain forest patiently observing bands of gorillas. It's quite likely, in fact, that we owe most conveniences of modernity and scientific insights about our world to someone else's indefatigable curiosity.

A two-sided coin

For these reasons, curiosity has long presented something of a puzzle to researchers. Over the past few decades of study and debate, psychologists have come up with a handful of different definitions, terms, and frameworks for curiosity, which generally fall into two main categories.

First, there's a spontaneous and ephemeral kind of curiosity, which over the years has been called *diversive*[1] or *exploratory*[2] curiosity. This kind of curiosity is typically triggered by external stimuli— something catches our fancy, providing us with an initial (and often impulsive) spark to explore our environment, an idea, or topic. When we experience this kind of curiosity, we may appear, in the words of researcher and cognitive psychologist Susan Engel, to be "inquisitive and interested." However, an overabundance of this kind of curiosity can cause a person to appear easily "distractible." Teachers and parents might even grow concerned that their students or children are using curiosity to "distract others and prevent focus."[3]

This fleeting kind of curiosity does not always serve a purpose. For example, we may wonder about a song lyric (are the Beach Boys really singing about "frying poultry in the sand"?) and go online for clarification (oh, *by a palm tree* in the sand"). Our initial curiosity, having led us to a website of misheard lyrics, could take us down a series of rabbit holes of other misheard lyrics. Thirty minutes or more may pass before we look at the clock and realize we've consumed valuable time following our curiosity, but not accomplished anything.

All of this, of course, is far different from the kind of sustained curiosity that leads to inventing light bulbs, developing a polio vaccine, or putting a man on the moon. This latter kind of curiosity entails sustained pursuit of challenging goals—a continued quest for knowledge even when the goal may seem elusive. We tend to admire this sort of curiosity, while harboring disdain for the other. This fact may explain some of our ambivalence about curiosity. We've all experienced that in one form, curiosity can be a vice, and in another form, a virtue.

Curiosity researchers call this deeper and more sustained kind of curiosity *specific* or *informational* curiosity. [4, 5] As the more focused and self-directed cousin of diversive curiosity, it reflects the need "to find ever more information on a particular topic." [6] Instead of flitting from one topic to the next, this second type of curiosity drives us to delve deeply into something and get smarter about it. It's often associated with inner drive to learn, stick-to-it-iveness, and relentless pursuit of knowledge just beyond our reach.

In sum, we might think of diversive curiosity as those fleeting impulses to learn that we experience while looking at tabloids in the supermarket checkout aisle or overhearing a juicy conversation in the booth next to us at a restaurant. Specific or informational curiosity, on the other hand, is the more admirable or noble drive to understand something deeply, to experiment doggedly, and to master complex knowledge.

That said, we shouldn't consider one kind of curiosity exclusively good and the other exclusively bad. Indeed, most people, according to researchers, display *both* kinds, albeit in differing levels of balance.

Moreover, these two kinds of curiosity can work hand-in-hand. Every expert began, of course, as a novice. First, they had to become interested in the topic, explore it a bit more, and eventually become engrossed in it. To pursue knowledge in depth, we need a spark of interest in the topic. Our natural human tendency, though, is to become less interested in something as we become more familiar with it.

Thus, we need new sparks of interest to stay engaged in our pursuits: To remain curious about something long enough to explore it deeply, we must continually find new wrinkles or surprises in it that make it feel new again, compelling us to dig deeper.

What sparks curiosity?

At this point, we might wonder (or, ahem, feel *curious* about), what exactly causes curiosity? Where does curiosity come from—how does it spring forth from our consciousness and spark our seemingly spontaneous impulses to learn? Over the years, numerous experiments have teased out the conditions that arouse curiosity—many of which we can easily reproduce in a classroom, staff meeting, conversation with a friend, or presentation to a large audience. Here's a starter list drawn from a synthesis conducted by one of the preeminent names in the field of curiosity research, George Loewenstein.[7]

◊ **Manageable knowledge gaps.** Fundamentally, we become curious when we experience a gap in our knowledge. That's why we're suckers for incomplete sequences (e.g., 1, 2, 3, 5, 8 . . . what comes next?) and unfinished narratives (e.g., a cliffhanger prior to a commercial break). Riddles and puzzles also fit into this category, especially when we have a "reference-point" with them.[8] We tend to become more interested in a topic when we a) know something about it, and b) feel our knowledge gap closing. This explains why it's much harder to put down a mystery novel five pages from the ending than five pages from the beginning.

◊ **Guessing, and receiving feedback.** To become curious about something, we must also become aware of our knowledge gap—that is, know that we *don't* know something. Studies have found, for example, that when we receive "accuracy feedback"—making a guess and learning we have guessed wrong—we want to learn the correct answer. In one study,[9] researchers found people became more interested to learn the *easternmost* state in the U.S. after they made a guess (and received accuracy feedback) about the *westernmost* state in the nation. (In case you're wondering, Alaska is both the easternmost and westernmost state in the U.S., as its Aleutian Islands cross into the eastern hemisphere.)

◊ **Incongruities.** We also become curious when we encounter something that doesn't fit our expectations. Consider, for example, the spark of curiosity you likely feel when you learn (or learned) that winds blowing down from mountaintops into valleys below can sometimes be *warm*, not cold, or that offering *fewer* flavor choices of jams in a supermarket display encourages people to buy *more* jars of jam. In both cases, you may find yourself wondering, why is that?

◊ **Controversy.** Researchers have also found that controversy begets curiosity. In a now famous experiment, researchers randomly assigned fifth- and sixth-grade students to work in groups. One group was instructed to engage in cooperative learning about a topic (for example, strip mining or designating wolves as an endangered species); the other was encouraged to focus on controversy in the topic. Students in the controversy condition demonstrated more interest in the topic, sought more information on it, and were more likely to give up a recess period to watch a film about it.[10]

◊ **Someone knows something we don't.** We might call this the "I have a secret" phenomenon. For example, a friend telling us they've bought a great present for us but won't tell us what it is until our birthday, or hearing someone sitting next to us chuckle while reading a magazine article are both apt to make us curious.

What all of this suggests is that there are a number of ways our external environment can arouse our curiosity.

Yet we might wonder about people who seem to be *perpetually* curious. They don't simply respond to stimuli, but rather, seem to spark *their own curiosity*. They're always asking questions, reading books, wondering about ideas, exploring new places, and meeting new people. That seems like a different, deeper, and more internalized form of curiosity than the fleeting variety triggered by conditions in our external environment.

It is.

These conditions (we might even say gimmicks) for creating curiosity are all fairly task-specific and reflect what researchers call *state* curiosity. Such ephemeral forms of curiosity are a far cry, of course, from the form of curiosity that comes to mind when we think of a Jane Goodall, Albert Einstein, or Marie Curie—people with insatiable intellectual appetites who keep asking questions. They're not just curious from time to time, but *always* curious. This kind of deeper, more internalized curiosity reflects what many researchers call *trait* curiosity.

Becoming curious people

It's *trait* curiosity that's most often linked to positive outcomes in school, the workplace, and life itself. Trait curiosity gives us a fire inside to keep learning, even in the face of challenges. People with high levels of trait curiosity are curious *as people*. We might think of it as the difference between an *-ing* or *-er* ending on verbs. It's one thing to say we're writing, swimming, singing, or inquiring, and something different to call ourselves *writers, swimmers, singers,* or *inquirers*. So, too, it's one thing to say I *feel* curious, and something different to say I *am* curious.

As we'll see throughout this book, it's this latter form of trait curiosity that's typically linked to better academic performance, relationships, job performance, and the like. New studies are finding, though, that trait curiosity itself is not a single, monolithic characteristic, but rather, takes different forms, including "joyous exploration" (seeking novel stimuli), "social curiosity" (seeking to understand others), "stress tolerance" (embracing ambiguity), "deprivation sensitivity" (focused problem solving), and "thrill seeking" (being open to novel and even risky experiences). [11] Although researchers continue to study (and debate) how to define and categorize curiosity, for our purposes it may be helpful to picture curiosity as sorting out like this:

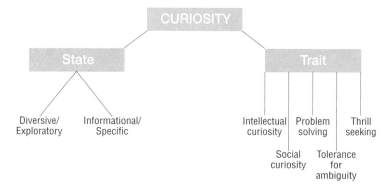

Creating these two big "buckets" of state and trait curiosity prompts a nature-versus-nurture question—specifically, is trait curiosity something innate, a personality characteristic (as the label might suggest), and accordingly, a product of nature? In other words, are some people naturally predisposed to be more curious than others?

Or, instead, is trait curiosity more of a discipline—something akin to a talent, like singing, that has elements of nature (some people are gifted with better vocal chords than others), but nevertheless, must be nurtured and developed?

The answer to this question has profound implications. If curiosity is in our stars (or genes) that would mean some people are born to be more curious—and thus to lead happier, more successful, and longer lives—while the rest of humanity is fated to toil away in a humdrum, incurious existence. If, on the other hand, curiosity is a trait we can *develop*, we ought to contemplate another question altogether, especially in light of the wide variance researchers observe in people's reported levels of curiosity: Why do so many people seem to *lose their curiosity* or struggle to rekindle it?

As we'll discover in the next chapter, our search for an answer to this question of whether curiosity is born more out of nature or nurture will take us on a winding road with a few surprises lurking around each corner.

CHAPTER TWO

Are We Naturally Curious?

In his book, *Dad is Fat*, comedian Jim Gaffigan, a father of five children, recounts the incessant questions young children ask.

> They learn to speak. And the questions commence. Anyone with kids knows about questions. "Daddy, what are you doing? Daddy, why are you doing that? Daddy, how long are you going to be doing that? Daddy, why are you putting on headphones and having a beer for breakfast?"[1]

The humor in Gaffigan's experiences reflects, of course, what anyone who's been around children for much time at all knows: They're full of questions. They're curious, incessantly (and at times annoyingly) so.

That's because, as cognitive psychologist John Medina has observed, human beings are hardwired to be curious.[2] Our natural propensity for curiosity, in fact, likely contributed to our ability to survive and thrive as a species—mastering fire, horticulture, shelter construction, hunting, and oceanic navigation—the list goes on and on. Human infants, Medina observes, are natural-born scientists; they are constantly exploring their environments, grasping for objects, and putting them in their mouths.

Nonetheless, as with most phenomena, researchers have observed that exactly how much curiosity infants demonstrate tends to vary. Some toddlers appear to be more prone to curiosity, demonstrating greater levels of what's called "stimulation seeking" (e.g., investigating new objects in their environments) than others. A longitudinal study of 1,795 children, for example, found that as three-year-olds, they demonstrated considerable variance in stimulation seeking; eight years later, those who had demonstrated greater stimulation seeking as toddlers scored 12 points higher on IQ tests than their lower stimulation-seeking peers.[3] At first blush, these findings might suggest that curiosity is ingrained, more a product of nature than nurture. Yet, as we'll see, the truth is actually far messier than that.

Observing curiosity in a "strange situation"

In 1954, Mary Ainsworth, a child psychologist and researcher, found herself in East Africa—an unexpected career twist after her husband, an anthropologist, was relocated to Uganda, compelling her to leave an enviable position at the famous Tavistock Clinic in London. She did so under one condition: that she could continue her own research, applying the rigorous observation techniques she learned at Tavistock to analyze the parenting practices of 26 mothers of newborns in six villages in the Kampala region of Uganda. Over nine months, she visited the mothers in their sparse homes, many with dirt floors, and watched them interact with their infants for two hours at a time every other week.

At first, the mothers were wary of her and her interpreter, but over time, they grew more comfortable with the strangers in their homes, allowing Ainsworth to observe their genuine interactions with their infant children. Before long, she noticed recurring patterns and distinct differences in those interactions, which led her to conclude that regardless of maternal age or wealth (almost all the mothers were young and poor) there were three types of mother-child relationships:

◊ Some babies were "**securely attached.**" They enjoyed close, mutually affectionate relationships with their mothers. They were content in the presence of their mothers, who served as safe harbors from which infants could venture out and explore their surroundings.

◊ Some babies were "**insecurely attached**." They were fretful (and often tearful) even in their mothers' presence, and rarely seemed to want to venture far from their mothers.

◊ Some babies were "**not yet attached**." They appeared to be indifferent to their mothers and to have weak bonds with them.

Eventually, Ainsworth moved to Baltimore, Maryland, where she continued to study mothers and their infants—and observed the same pattern among them. In 1970, she began a now-famous line of research with 100 pairs of mothers and infants called the "strange situation" studies. Ainsworth would invite a mother and child to a room filled with toys. While the mother sat silently in a chair, the infant would explore the toys in the room. After a few minutes, a stranger would enter the room and begin talking to the mother, then approach the infant, offering him or her a toy. While the infant was distracted, the mother would exit the room, leaving the infant alone with the stranger.

Usually, the infant would remain so engrossed with the toy that he or she wouldn't notice the mother's absence until a few minutes later, when the mother would return to the room; at that moment, the infant realized that they had been left alone with a stranger. And that's when the interesting part of the experiment began. In most cases, the mother's return—and the child's realization they'd been left alone—would cause the infant to become upset and seek consolation from the mother.

About 70 percent of the time, after a bit of consoling and drying of tears, the child would again feel comfortable, leave the mother's lap, and return to exploring the room and the toys in it. Some infants (about 10 percent), however, would remain distraught for several minutes—or even start screaming and hitting their mothers. Afterward, they would remain close to their mothers, showing little or no inclination to return to exploring the room or playing with the toys in it. A third group of children (about 20 percent) showed almost no emotion or attachment to their mothers—regardless of whether they were in the room.

As it turns out, the patterns in children's reactions to the stranger in the room mapped closely onto the bonds they had formed with their mothers. Just as Ainsworth had observed in Uganda, the mothers in Baltimore who demonstrated sensitivity to, and warmth with, their children appeared to provide them with a safe harbor from which they could venture out and explore their worlds. Conversely, children who remained distraught and were reluctant to reengage in exploring the room had mothers who were inconsistent in their interactions with their children—for example, intermittently consoling them and admonishing them for their lack of independence. And finally, the children who showed a willingness to explore the room, but demonstrated little bond with or interest in others, typically had mothers who were standoffish and detached, sometimes ignoring their children altogether.

Nurturing curiosity

Ainsworth's findings suggest that environmental conditions—in this case, how mothers interact with their children—have a profound influence on infants' desire to explore their worlds, or in a word, their *curiosity*. Replication studies of the "strange situation" experiment from around the world have confirmed the importance of nurture when it comes to curiosity. These studies have found, for example, cultural patterns of parenting and corresponding differences in how children respond to being left alone with a stranger. For example, in Germany, where mothering styles favor non-clinging children, more than twice as many children (49 percent) as in the U.S. demonstrated detachment from their mothers,[4] which would suggest that children's sense of security is not solely a reflection of their temperament, but also the environment and caregiving they receive and the broader cultural milieu in which they live.

Certainly, there are some who debate this point, speculating, for example, that children's inherent temperaments might dictate their behavior in these studies.[5] However, some empirical studies appear to disprove this assertion; they first measured children's temperament types, then observed them in "stranger situations" and found the children's personalities had far less to do with their behavior than their mothers' parenting styles.[6, 7]

At this point, we might wonder if people's level of curiosity gets programmed in (or squeezed out) at an early age and stays at that level for the rest of their lives. To some extent, how we're raised likely influences how much openness to new ideas and experiences we demonstrate later in life. Yet several interesting experiments suggest that regardless of where people's curiosity dials are set, some relatively simple (and often subtle) tweaks to their environments can ignite their curiosity—tapping into their natural desire to explore, find pleasure in novelty, and experience the joy of discovery.

Creating curiosity conditions

Over the years, many studies have confirmed that environmental conditions—including how other adults (not just parents) interact with children—significantly influence their openness to exploration. For example, a study of 40 preschool children found that children were more apt to explore their surroundings in the presence of a friendly, supportive adult than in the company of an aloof, critical one. [8] In another study, adults were directed to interact with students in three different ways:

◊ Answering students' questions with only brief, direct responses to encourage their *independence.*

◊ Demonstrating *active interest* in students' curiosity by encouraging their inquisitiveness with smiles and eye contact and attentiveness.

◊ *Focusing* their interest by asking pointed follow-up questions to encourage further exploration of topics.

The latter two conditions—demonstrating active interest and focusing children's interest—were found to support more exploratory behavior, especially among children whose teachers or parents had initially identified them as having low levels of curiosity.[9] This last point is important because it suggests that kids' curiosity is not *solely* a function of parenting or maternal bonds; even brief interaction with other adults can help kids find and unleash curiosity within themselves.

In a more recent study, Tessa van Schijndel and her colleagues sent preschool children into a children's museum under three different conditions: 1) an adult accompanying the children would offer minimal interaction beyond a few words of encouragement, 2) the adult would elaborate on what the children did, providing them with some thought-provoking questions, and 3) the adult would assume the role of teacher, explaining the whys and hows of the exhibits (in this case, rolling cylinders of different sizes down a ramp or experiencing centrifugal forces while sitting in a spinning chair). As it turns out, the third style of adult interaction (explaining the exhibits to students) seemed to backfire; children spent the least amount of time investigating the exhibits when adults explained the phenomena they demonstrated to them, seemingly removing the mystery.[10]

Several years ago, Susan Engel, a preeminent researcher of children's curiosity, replicated an earlier study to determine which has more of an effect on children's curiosity: genetic or parental pre-programming, or the environment in which they find themselves— in this case, their school classrooms. For the study, Engel and her colleague, Hilary Hackmann, placed a "curiosity box"—a wooden cabinet with 18 drawers containing novelty items—in different classrooms, accompanied with a sign that read, "Okay to touch."

Then, they quietly observed the classrooms to see how students would interact with it, how many students would approach the box, and how many drawers they'd open to experience the joy of discovering the tiny surprises inside. If curiosity were simply a matter of genetics or parental programming, we might expect to see every classroom reflect a similar bell curve of variable interactions with the box: Some children would fully engage with it, opening every drawer; some might be mildly interested in it, trying a few drawers; and others would ignore it altogether.

Yet that's not what Engel and Hackmann found. Instead, they observed variability among classrooms: That is, in some classrooms, many students actively engaged with the box. Upon seeing the box in the back of their classrooms, they would say things like, "What is that?" "Whoa, where did that come from?" and "It says OK to touch, so I'm going to touch it."[11]

In other classrooms, students hardly touched the box. Why was that? As it turns out, the critical link was "how much the teacher smiled and talked in an encouraging manner and the level of curiosity children in the room expressed."[12] Engel and Hackmann, in fact, found a direct link between the number of smiles and encouraging words the teachers offered and students' exploration of the curiosity box. In classrooms where students explored the box, teachers would say things like, "What do you have there? Wow, I think you really like that thing. That's cool. Look at that." Meanwhile, in classrooms where students would ignore the box, teachers would say things like, "Rachel, turn your body around and do your work" (i.e., stop looking at the box), or "I saw some of you up there by the box, and you owe me Friday's English."

A curious childhood

Decades ago, Mildred Goertzel, a teacher of emotionally disturbed children, and her husband Victor Goertzel, a clinical psychologist, found themselves in the embarrassing position of not knowing what to do about their eldest of three sons, Ted, a smart child who was underachieving in school and having difficulty making friends.[13] It was the late 1950s, and not much was known about gifted children like Ted—nor were there any support groups or websites from which to glean information. So, Mildred went to the local library, and walking past the shelves of books on psychology and child development (she already knew plenty about both topics), she began looking for biographies of famous, gifted people who had made special contributions throughout history and who she hoped might serve as role models for her sons.

As she consumed the biographies of hundreds of luminaries, including Martin Luther King, Jr., Eleanor Roosevelt, Winston Churchill, Mahatma Gandhi, and Theodore Roosevelt, and shared them with her husband, they realized she had unearthed a treasure trove of information overlooked by most researchers. They decided to write a book together—not for academics and educators, but for parents like themselves who were struggling to raise gifted children. Over the next few decades, the Goertzels and their son Ted would scour hundreds of biographies of famous people and report their findings in several books that would identify some peculiar common themes among these famous people's childhood experiences. [14]

The first thing to jump off the pages of these biographies was that the childhood homes of these distinguished individuals all reflected a love for learning and a persistent drive toward ambitious goals. That much perhaps was to be expected. What was less expected, though, was that many of these high achievers also spent considerable time *out of school*, exploring their environments. Fully four-fifths of them showed great promise in school, yet *three-fifths* of them expressed dissatisfaction with their school experiences, apparently gaining far more from their own academic exploration, which was often supported by tutoring from their parents or others.

In other words, the greatest achievers in history were often *unschooled* as much as they were schooled. Given what we now know about how schooling so often tends to quash curiosity and (as we'll see throughout this book) how powerful curiosity is for fueling lifelong success, it perhaps only stands to reason that the world's most influential people spent much of their childhoods learning independently—although often with the aid of a mentor who let them *explore* their environments. It's an insight that bears repeating—great achievers had time to explore their environments. They were not *forced* to learn; rather, they had freedom of choice to find their own sparks of interest and fan them into flames of sustained interest.

Curiosity, as it turns out, cannot be forced. We cannot *make* students become curious; rather, we must lead them to it by creating environments and opportunities for curiosity to flourish.

What all of this suggests is that curiosity isn't taught or compelled, but, rather, emerges like a sprouting plant when the conditions are right. In short, the environments we create for children—at home, in school, and elsewhere—can cause curiosity to flourish or fade. And, as we'll see later in this book, the same appears to be true for adults: The workplaces, relationships, and communities in which we immerse ourselves can either summon or *suppress* our curiosity.

These insights might lead us to another question: What exactly is going on in our brains when we're curious? Why are *spontaneous* sparks of interest so essential to learning? Can we learn *without* being curious? Here, a whole new generation of neuroscience is enabling researchers to peer into our brains—often at the precise moment that sparks of curiosity occur—and in so doing, reveal the exact parts of our brains that fire in an explosion of chemicals when we're curious.

Through this modern science, we're finding that curiosity is a Sherpa of sorts for new knowledge, shouldering new ideas down a long and perilous journey to a final destination in our long-term memories. Sure, learning can happen *without* curiosity, but like a mountain climber without a guide, it's more apt to get lost along the way when curiosity is absent.

On top of that, as we'll see, satisfying our curiosity—closing those nagging gaps in our knowledge—floods our brains with "feel good" chemicals, so much so that it seems entirely possible to develop an "addiction" to seeking and finding new knowledge. In other words, we can be addicted to exploration, discovery, and novelty.

And what exactly do we call these addicts? We call them *curious*, of course. 💡

CHAPTER THREE

This Is Your Brain on Curiosity

Imagine, for a moment, that you're working in an ice cream parlor that serves only two types of ice cream, chocolate or vanilla. To expedite service, you've been asked to predict customers' orders based solely on clues provided by their appearance. Your customers, as it turns out, are Mr. Potato Head dolls, and their physical features consist of a handful of permutations of bow tie, moustache, glasses, and hat.

By this point, you've probably figured out you're playing a game—one designed by a team of researchers in Massachusetts who want to find out what exactly happens in our brains during cliffhanger moments of suspense while we're awaiting a resolution to our curiosity.[1] During the study, images of different "customers" (i.e., different versions of Mr. Potato Head) appear in front of your eyes for a few seconds and you're asked to press one of two buttons, representing chocolate or vanilla, to make your prediction. Afterward, the screen goes dark for a few seconds (building suspense) before flashing an answer: Mr. Potato Head holding either a chocolate or vanilla ice cream cone.

After repeated guesses and feedback, you start to get better, detecting the pattern and getting more right answers after those tantalizing moments of suspense. When you get the correct answer, you feel a buzz of elation in your brain, like the *ding! ding! ding!* of hitting a jackpot on a slot machine. Throughout the whole experiment, your brain has been connected to an imaging device that provides a fascinating insight to researchers conducting the study: During that brief moment when you learned you guessed the correct answer, your brain activated a reward center that releases dopamine into your system.

Because dopamine provides the sensation of pleasure, it's also at the root of many habits and addictions—both bad and good—which means that the intellectual exercise of satisfying our curiosity is likely to be habit forming. When we feel curious, we want to satisfy our curiosity because we know that when we do, we'll experience a little moment of joy. As a result, we begin to crave it.

Making memories stick

Brain science also reveals that, in addition to creating a positive craving, the more curiosity drives our learning, the more likely we are to recall what we've learned later. As researchers at the University of California, Davis, discovered in an unusual experiment,[2] simply being in a state of heightened curiosity makes us more susceptible to learning new knowledge—even information irrelevant to what sparked our initial curiosity.

Here's how the study worked. Initially, the researchers asked participants to review a list of trivia questions (What does the term "dinosaur" really mean? Who was president of the U.S. when Uncle Sam first got a beard?) and indicate how likely they were to know the answer and how curious each question made them. In a second phase of the study, the participants reread the questions that were now divided into two sets—those that made them curious and those that did not. After each question, the study participants viewed an image of a person's face for 14 seconds before finally learning the answer to the trivia question—all while having their brains scanned by an imaging device.

A day later, the study participants returned to the lab and the researchers quizzed them on not only the right answers to the questions, but also the faces they had seen. As it turns out, the participants could better recall both the answers to questions for which they reported higher levels of curiosity *as well as* the irrelevant images of people's faces that had preceded answers to their questions. In short, curiosity seems to have primed their brains for learning and knowledge retention. Brain scans confirmed this: When participants reported being curious, their brains' dopamine-releasing reward centers were activated, followed by increased activity in the hippocampus, which is involved in the creation of memories.

Curiouser and curiouser

In light of the addictive nature of curiosity, a similar phenomenon may be at play in what reading researchers have called the Matthew effect, named for the passage in the Gospel of Matthew that refers to the rich getting richer and the poor getting poorer. Studies have shown that students who are more capable of reading find it more enjoyable, and thus read more and become even better (richer) readers, while poor readers tend to read less and thus become, in relative terms, even poorer readers.[3]

When it comes to curiosity, the curious may become curiouser, and the incurious may become *less* curious, or simply bored. Recall that curiosity is associated with dopamine spikes in our brains—the same chemical that gets released when we encounter any kind of novel event, be it seeing a new movie, hearing a funny joke, pleasing our taste buds, or experiencing our first kiss. However, we also know from brain research that novel events produce diminishing returns when it comes to dopamine. Thus, as we encounter the same stimuli over and over (a process known as habituation), our dopamine levels decrease—which explains why songs grow tiresome after too many hearings, jokes get old after too much repeating, eating the same thing for lunch every day loses its pleasure, and romance can fade months or years after that first kiss. It also explains why, to *remain* curious about something (or someone), we need to continually ask new questions and make new discoveries—like discovering a new favorite musical artist, finding new recipes for lunchtime salads and sandwiches, or learning that our long-term romantic partner also likes piña coladas and getting caught in the rain (hat tip to Rupert Holmes).

The point here is that our brains are hardwired to seek new stimuli—the question is *which* stimuli will we use to fill that need? As we'll see in later chapters, curious people learn to satisfy their thirst for novelty through intellectual stimulation—for example, continually expanding the repertoire of songs they play on the guitar or developing deeper relationships with their romantic partners. The less curious, on the other hand, who haven't trained their brains to crave intellectual stimulation, may seek it through physical or chemical stimulation, or self-destructive behaviors. Indeed, counselors often find that boredom lies at the heart of many drug addictions; teaching addicts to overcome boredom through more constructive novelty seeking is often the key to avoiding relapse.[4]

The curious nature of curiosity research

A caveat: As we move beyond neuroscientific studies of the brain and dig deeper into research on curiosity, we'll plunge into what some view as the spongy center of a great deal of social science and psychology research: self-report data and correlational findings. As with many measures of personality and thinking styles, researchers continue to debate the accuracy of curiosity scales, often because of their reliance on asking people to self-report personal preferences and/or their daily behaviors—which requires that their subjects provide honest and accurate answers.

Nonetheless, as we'll see throughout this book, these surveys do generate a wide array of results, which suggests people responding to them seem to do so honestly, revealing what would appear to be genuine differences in their dispositions and behavior. Researchers can thus compare these variances in self-reported curiosity with other data, like academic learning, job performance, and interpersonal relationships, and in so doing arrive at some intriguing and often surprising conclusions.

At the same time, it's worth noting that as we dive into research on curiosity, we'll also encounter what can be a frustrating fluidity of terminology and concepts. Already, you may be wondering: Why are there two terms, diversive and exploratory, and not just one, to describe the same sort of curiosity? Candidly, one reason for this is likely the "publish-or-perish" reality of academia, where researchers are more apt to make a name for themselves by creating their own frameworks and models than by latching onto someone else's concepts or replicating their studies. Another reason, though, is that we're talking about the complex inner workings of the human mind and even more complex relationships of people to their environments—things we cannot subject to the same sort of empirical research as, say, giving an experimental group a dose of medicine and a control group a sugar-pill placebo. So, we're left with researchers' earnest attempts to connect dots and make sense of best available data and their resulting theories and frameworks.

In the end, curiosity may remain an abstract concept that we can never completely pin down, leaving us with insights that may feel like we're trying to make sense of the shadows on the wall in Plato's famous Allegory of the Cave—more a reflection of reality than a precise measure of it. Nonetheless, if we can accept the inherent squishiness of some of this research and keep our minds open to the metaphors, constructs, and theories that researchers use to encircle a complex and messy phenomenon, we can arrive together at some compelling insights about the nature of curiosity, which, in turn, can have some profound implications for us and our happiness. 💡

PART II

Curiosity in School

"Kids are born curious about the world. What adults primarily do in the presence of kids is unwittingly thwart the curiosity of children."

–Neil deGrasse Tyson

CHAPTER FOUR

Quashing Curiosity

One snowy morning not so long ago, I met my youngest daughter Molly, who was then in first grade (about the same time she quizzed me on fluorescent lighting), coming down the stairs on her way to breakfast while I was going upstairs to get ready for work.

"Is this a school day?" she asked.

With a snow falling outside in a late spring snowstorm (common in Colorado, where we live), I figured she was hoping for a snow day. "Yes, you still have school today," I informed her, expecting her shoulders to slump dejectedly.

Instead, she pumped her fist and exclaimed, "Yes!"

As a parent, I was elated; my child was happy *it wasn't* a snow day. As it happens, Molly's excitement about going to school had bubbled straight out of her curiosity; the day before, her class had begun an overnight science experiment and she couldn't wait to return to school to see what had happened.

While driving my other daughters to school that morning, I asked Emma, in middle school at the time, how she felt about going to school. "Sleepy, but excited," she said before listing a couple interesting things in store for her, including an "invention convention" project she was busily preparing for her school science fair. I asked my eldest daughter, Sophie, then in high school, if she shared Molly's excitement for school. "Yes, I'm super excited," she responded, but with wry teenage sarcasm. Eventually, she allowed that she *was* excited to be playing in a tennis meet that afternoon (providing the snow melted), having just joined the junior varsity team.

Turning talent and interest into boredom

As parents, we'd like to imagine that when we send our kids off to school, they'll be entering environments that challenge them to learn what they need to be successful in life, as well as spark their interest in learning. Yet the pattern I saw in my own daughters that morning reflects national trends—the longer students stay in school, the less intrinsic motivation they report in their core subjects. According to a longitudinal study of more than 100 students (called the Fullerton Study), while high schoolers remain interested in *school* overall, their engagement is bolstered largely by extracurriculars, which overshadows their waning interest in regular classes.[1]

More than two decades ago, Mihaly Csikszentmihalyi (pronounced *cheek-sent-me-high*) and his colleagues discovered much the same phenomenon when he set out to determine why some teenagers nurture their talents and others do not[2]—a study of what we might call the high school yearbook paradox. We probably all know someone from school who everyone assumed would accomplish great things, be it in sports, music, arts, business, or politics. Years later, though, we may have bumped into them on the street, caught up with them at a reunion, or found them on Facebook and been surprised to see they hadn't realized their early potential—they didn't move to Hollywood, become a sports star, or become a rocket scientist like everyone had assumed. Conversely, we've probably all had classmates who unexpectedly achieved some form of success or even stardom in their chosen fields; somehow, they took a dormant or nascent talent and doggedly cultivated it, surprising more than a few people along the way.

The question that Csikszentmihalyi and his colleagues sought to answer was: What does it take for teenagers to nurture their talents and interests long enough to develop true expertise? For the study, they found 208 teenagers identified by teachers as having exceptional promise in art, music, mathematics, science, or athletics, and set out to see how they spent their days and what they did, or did not do, to cultivate their talents. Using the technology of the day—pagers—they pinged students at random intervals throughout the day and asked them to record what they were doing and their level of engagement while doing it.

Specifically, they were curious whether the students' school experiences offered any periods of optimal motivation required to cultivate talents—a condition Csikszentmihalyi had earlier dubbed "flow," a sort of Cinderella-at-the-ball experience marked by "losing track of time and being unaware of fatigue and of everything else but the activity itself."[3]

The resulting in-depth portrait of the teenagers' lives offers a gloomy picture of high school life, which likely hasn't changed much since then. While in class, most students reported high levels of concentration but low levels of interest, even in subjects in which they were highly skilled. In many classrooms, teachers seemed to leech joy from learning by not explaining its purpose or applying it to the outside world. As one talented yet disappointed math student noted, "Once you have the theorem down, it would help you to know how you could use it, instead of just strictly what it is. I think it makes it more interesting and easier to learn."[4]

Bored to death

Csikszentmihalyi's observations are reflected in other studies as well, which have found that the longer children stay in school, the less curiosity they demonstrate or are encouraged to demonstrate. To wit: In his studies of school-age children dating back to the 1960s, creativity researcher Paul Torrance found that while teachers said they viewed curiosity as important, they typically did not identify their *best* students as those who demonstrated curiosity.[5] Moreover, while 72 percent of elementary teachers said they valued students' unusual questions, only 42 percent of middle school said likewise.[6]

A study in the 1980s found a similar pattern of declining emphasis on student curiosity among classroom teachers. In 2nd and 3rd grades, fully 65 percent of teachers surveyed reported that they encouraged curiosity in their classrooms. Yet in 4th and 5th grades, that number had dropped to 41 percent of teachers.[7] In a follow-up study of 298 students in 3rd, 5th, and 7th grades enrolled in a predominantly white Catholic school in a working-class neighborhood and a predominantly black public school in the Midwestern U.S., researchers found the same pattern: In both settings, school-related curiosity decreased as children grew older.[8]

Through her series of classroom observations, Susan Engel, whom we met earlier with her studies of students' interactions with the "curiosity box," found kindergarten students displaying, on average, 2.36 episodes of curiosity over a two-hour period.[9] By 5th grade, however, that number had dropped to 0.48 episodes in a two-hour period, which suggests that many children spend their entire school day "without asking even one question or engaging in one sequence of behavior aimed at finding out something new."[10] And by the time students reach high school, surveys have found that nearly two-thirds of students (65 percent) report being bored in class on a daily basis, with just 2 percent reporting never feeling bored; the top two reasons they cite for being bored is that classroom material is uninteresting (82 percent) or not personally relevant to them (41 percent).[11]

No time for curiosity

Granted, high school boredom is hardly a new phenomenon; we probably all have some flashbacks of high school tedium and chuckle when we see Ben Stein's deadpan lecture in *Ferris Bueller's Day Off.* Yet that ought to strike us as odd. After all, given the close links among curiosity, learning, and memory, our schools ought to be rife with curiosity—especially as students reach higher levels of learning where they should be learning science that unravels the mysteries of the universe, experiencing great literature that provides insights into the human condition, and learning mathematics that can solve complex real-life problems. But instead, many classrooms appear to be completely misaligned with what sparks curiosity. For example, video comparisons with other countries find that when it comes to mathematics instruction, American teachers commonly downgrade complex problems into simple tasks, turning intriguing and curiosity-evoking challenges—like figuring out how to calculate the area of a triangle—into spoon-fed formulas.[12] American teachers seem to be in such a rush to cut to the chase and *give* students the right answer, that students experience little of the joy (or critical thinking) that comes from wrapping their minds around challenging problems and working out the right answer.[13]

In other words, fellow educators, many of us are designing and delivering classroom lessons in a manner that runs counter to what we know about how curiosity is sparked and sustained. Or as cognitive scientist John Medina has observed, "If you wanted to create an education environment that was directly opposed to what the brain was good at doing, you probably would design something like a classroom."[14]

Yet before we pile on teachers and blame them for creating humdrum classrooms, we might consider the observation attributed to various organizational theorists, including W. Edwards Deming, Don Berwick, and Paul Batalden: "Every system is perfectly designed to get the result that it does."[15] So if our schools and classrooms are tedious places, void of engagement and curiosity, it's quite possible that it's because we've historically designed them to be that way. In many ways, as we'll see, boring students to death may be an unintended consequence of a three-decade effort to grab American schools by the collar and shake them out of what, at the time, was seen as the scourge of U.S. education: lackadaisical students, complacent teachers, and rampant mediocrity.

CHAPTER FIVE

Engineered for Boredom

Roughly 35 years ago, America stood at a crossroads. A Reagan administration report ominously titled *A Nation at Risk* had sounded the alarm that our schools had grown so complacent in accepting a "rising tide of mediocrity" for student learning that our national security now hung in the balance. "If an unfriendly foreign power had attempted to impose on America the mediocre educational performance that exists today," the report intoned, "we might well have viewed it as an act of war."[1]

Some rejected the report's hyperbolic rhetoric and accused the authors of selectively using data to create a "manufactured crisis."[2] Researchers at Sandia Laboratory in New Mexico, for example, dug deeply into the same data and arrived at the opposite conclusion: Student achievement had *increased in every subgroup* but overall averages were flat or declining due to more students being invited to take these tests. Those data, however, didn't see the light of day until almost 10 years later,[3] and by then policymakers on both sides of the aisle had busied themselves with bold efforts to "fix" our schools.

As a first step, 49 governors from across the U.S. gathered in Charlottesville, Virginia, in 1989, and in a rare moment of bipartisan camaraderie agreed to set goals for dramatically improving the performance of America's schools, starting with raising the bar for students, which quickly translated into setting new, higher standards for learning. That much seemed to make sense. Yet as these things go, the standards themselves often reflected Mark Twain's quip about a camel being a horse created by committee. From the outset, the standards were often too vague and too voluminous to clarify for teachers what exactly they ought to be teaching; by one estimate, teaching all the standards contained in various state and national association documents would take 22 years.[4]

Soon after, states rushed to adopt new tests to measure how well students were meeting the standards. Of course, with standards too numerous to teach, the tests quickly became the de facto curriculum for many schools and districts—a phenomenon known as "teaching to the test." Moreover, states increasingly took a "tough love" approach with schools, adopting sanctions and rewards to incentivize them to take the new standards and assessments seriously—an approach codified into law with the passage of the No Child Left Behind Act in 2001.

The performance pressure cooker

Basically, the prevailing theory of action behind these changes was this: Our schools (and by extension, the leaders, teachers, and students in them) were too lax and needed to be whipped back into shape. And because educators had supposedly gotten us into this mess in the first place, they couldn't be trusted with making schools better on their own, so states and federal officials needed to step up and demand results . . . *or else*. And so, we embarked down the path of using *external* motivators—namely high-stakes testing (that is, assessments with consequences for poor performance, which eventually included school closures and the termination of principals and teachers) to stem the supposed "rising tide of mediocrity."

Over time, what began as testing in just a couple of subjects every few years as a "dipstick" measure of performance turned into annual assessments in multiple subjects. With so much riding on test scores, district administrators were anxious to know which schools might be headed for trouble, so they could "support" them (or further ratchet up the pressure). School leaders also wanted to know which individual students and classrooms were struggling so they, too, could intervene with those students (which at times took the form of nudging them to drop out or classifying them as special needs so they could be exempted from taking the test). As a result of this proliferation of assessments, by 2014, students in many districts were taking 20 or more standardized tests per year.[5]

To make sure everyone was fully paying attention to student performance on the tests, federal policy encouraged states to rate teacher and school leader performance using hyper-complex formulas that were often weighted heavily toward student performance on the state test (as an example, New York City's system for rating teacher performance was concocted from 32 variables and spit out numerical ratings that few people fully understood).[6] Worse, the test-score-derived teacher ratings were often grossly inaccurate, as researchers at Mathematica Policy Research discovered when they analyzed data for so-called "value-added" models that measured student performance year-over-year and then assigned a numeric value to teacher performance. They found that even when three years of data were used, the error rate was still 25 percent—meaning that for every three teachers correctly "measured," another one was *incorrectly* measured.[7]

Consider the unfortunate case of Pascale Mauclair, a 6th-grade teacher at highly rated P.S. 11 in Queens. When the New York City Department of Education released its Teacher Data Reports in February 2012, they ranked Mauclair as one of the city's worst teachers. There was just one problem: It wasn't true. From the outset, the data were suspect: Of the seven 6th-grade teachers in P.S. 11, three received zero percentile scores—unlikely in a school rated in the 94th percentile of the city's public schools. Mauclair taught both math and English language arts to, primarily, small classes of immigrant students who were learning English and entered her classroom at different times during the year, with some taking the exam after just a few months in her class. Because of the small class size, the number of her students who took the language arts assessment was below the minimum for publicly reporting scores. Her rating as a teacher was thus based solely on the results for the 11 students who took the mathematics exam, a small sample prone to distortions.[8] Mauclair, a veteran teacher held in high regard with her peers, found reporters from the *New York Post* at her door, asking her what it was like to be such a terrible teacher.

So it's no surprise that teachers and principals alike report rising stress levels,[9] resulting in staff churn as they flee the profession.[10] At the same time, as test preparation has increasingly become the focus of classroom teaching, students drop out of school because they don't see how what they're learning—information which helps them score well on a standardized test—is relevant to them.[11] Nonetheless, we respond by wishing they had more "grit" to power through all of the meaningless tasks we throw at them.[12]

Diminishing returns

Some might argue that some of this "shock treatment" was needed; after all, we live in a competitive global economy, so we need to make sure our students can hold their own against their counterparts in other developing nations, right? Perhaps. Yet we might ask ourselves: Hold their own *doing what?* Moreover, when we step back to examine the actual impact of these three decades of attempts to "reform" schools, we see that across the U.S., as the shock of "get tough" accountability wears off, states and districts have hit performance plateaus.[13] A recent review of 17 years of performance data determined that adopting better standards and test-driven accountability resulted in some incremental performance gains among the lowest-achieving students in the lowest-performing states, but did little to improve overall student performance.[14] And it remains unclear whether standards and test-driven accountability did anything to create more consistent, higher-quality instruction; one study a decade into such reform efforts found that only 7 percent of students benefited from strong teaching over three years.[15]

Thus it may not be surprising that on international comparisons, despite the (perhaps misguided) hand-wringing about our standing against other nations that sent us down this path, the U.S. has seen only small increases as other nations have surpassed us,[16] often by following very different paths to reform.[17] While we in the U.S. have been using high-stakes testing to drive system improvements, leading performers such as the city of Shanghai and the countries of Singapore and Finland have dramatically changed their focus from *teaching facts* to *deeper learning*, from narrowly focused curricula to personalized learning for students, and away from high-stakes test performance as the sole goal of education to the development of well-rounded graduates with highly honed cognitive and non-cognitive skills and intelligences.[18] In a word, they've sought to help their students become *curious*.

Stepping back to ask bigger questions

So, it seems that as a nation we've devoted countless resources, time, and energy to creating a Rube Goldberg-esque system of top-down reform while overlooking something vitally important: Do our students care about any of this at all? Case in point: A team of economists led by Steven Levitt (of *Freakonomics* fame) found that a simple $10 incentive—introduced on the *day of the test*—persuaded students to take the high-stakes tests more seriously and resulted in a performance bump equivalent to *six months* of additional learning.[19] Although Levitt and his team congratulated themselves for "proving" that external rewards could significantly boost student performance, it seems they inadvertently uncovered something else: how little effort students typically put into these tests in the first place—the very tests, mind you, by which their schools and teachers were often being held accountable.

Let that sink in for a moment: Not only are we using complex, convoluted, and inaccurate formulas for judging school and teacher performance, but the very basis of those measures—student scores on standardized tests—appear to be suspect, given that they can be so easily manipulated with a mere $10 bribe.

Still, some may ask: But don't we need things like test score data to guide decision making? After all, businesses must operate with an eye on the bottom line, so why not schools? Yes, absolutely, schools need data, and to focus on student learning. That much is true. And it's also true that like any enterprise, schools should engage in continuous improvement—especially given the increasingly competitive global economy our students are entering—and the fact that many students still fail to graduate from school or to develop the skills they need to thrive in a modern economy.

Yet, even if we set aside for the moment the issue of whether standardized tests really measure student learning in any deep way, including their ability to apply knowledge to solve complex problems, create and defend logical arguments, and employ critical thinking skills, we might step back and ask a larger question: How should we *respond* to these data? That is, how should we motivate people to *use* the data to do *better*?

The approach we've taken for the past three decades is predicated on the notion that good old-fashioned carrots and sticks work best. We might call this the "or else" approach. Get better, *or else*. Get the job done, *or else* you're fired. Meet your quota, *or else* forfeit your commission.

The trouble with this approach, as a growing number of companies are discovering, is that it often doesn't motivate the right behaviors, especially when creativity and ingenuity are required to achieve better performance. In fact, Microsoft discovered that its "rank and yank" approach to performance evaluations—grading employees on a curve and dismissing the lowest performers—had led to a decade of stagnation and lack of innovation.[20] Meanwhile, successful businesses, like Gore-Tex, Toyota, Southwest Airlines, Apple, and Google, long ago abandoned their "or else" approaches and found, instead, that it's far more motivating to provide people with a sense of purpose, increase their autonomy and personal responsibility, and encourage their growth as individuals.[21]

High stress, low curiosity

The stress many educators face right now inhibits their ability to create the kind of learning environments that foster curiosity and student engagement. In such an environment, where educators' jobs hang in the balance if their students don't do well on tests that students themselves seemingly care little about, it's easy for teachers to feel like student curiosity is a luxury they simply cannot afford. Unleashing student curiosity takes time—something teachers often feel is in short supply when facing an externally mandated press to cover many curricular standards before year's end.

While observing children interacting with curiosity boxes in their classrooms, Susan Engel developed deep appreciation and sympathy for harried teachers, many of whom she saw under enormous pressure to cover vast amounts of material with "very specific objectives for each stretch of time," leading them to "put a great deal of effort into keeping children on task and reaching those objectives."[22]

During their studies of talented teachers, Csikszentmihalyi and his colleagues observed much the same thing: Teachers weren't entirely to blame for disengaged students. The schools and classrooms they were observing in the early 1990s had just been introduced to the rapidly spreading "reform" of standards-based curricula and assessments. "An unfortunate by-product of the standardized curricula in most modern schools," they observed, "is the depreciation of the role of teacher to that of information technician."[23] Many teachers in the study appeared to be mechanically plodding through the curriculum, teaching what must be taught with little effort to explain its meaning or purpose. On the other hand, in both Csikszentmihalyi's study and longitudinal studies of student motivation,[24] even as high school students were reporting declining interest in their core subjects, they also reported rising interest in arts, music, and extracurricular pursuits (which, perhaps not incidentally, remained free from the yoke of standardized testing).

Consider another experiment that Susan Engel and her colleague, Kellie Randall, conducted with teachers who were tasked with guiding individual students through a science experiment supported by a worksheet.[25] For one group of teachers and students, the researcher left the room by saying, "Have fun learning about science!"

For the other group, the researcher said, "Have fun doing the worksheet!"

As it turns out, Engel and Randall weren't studying *students*, as the teachers had been led to believe, but rather, they were studying the *teachers* themselves. The researchers had recruited students to serve as their confederates, telling them beforehand to intentionally alter the experiment by picking up a piece of candy (instead of a raisin as directed on the worksheet) and dropping it into a liquid with the shrugging explanation, "I just wanted to see what would happen."

And what happened at that point was, indeed, interesting. The teachers who'd been given the parting thought to have fun *learning about science* were far more likely to encourage the students' further exploration, even suggesting other objects the students might drop into the liquid. But the second group of teachers, those who had been told to have fun *doing the worksheet,* were more apt to try to get students back on task, redirecting them back to the instructions on the worksheet and stifling their exploration.

If such a simple reframing of a single learning task could so profoundly impact how teachers interact with students in a laboratory experiment, we might wonder how regular reminders for teachers to cover everything on the test is likely to influence how they interact with students and in turn, suppress student curiosity. Conversely, we might wonder what regular reminders to *have fun learning* could do for creating classrooms where students and their curiosity can flourish.

Let's pause a moment to wonder what it might look like if were to roll back the clock and return to the crossroads we faced as nation in the 1980s. This time, instead of taking the path toward high-stakes testing, hyper-complex formulas for measuring school and teacher performance, and castigating educators for failing to get their students to perform well on bubble-sheet exams, let's instead consider what might have been—and still could be—if we were to take a different path, one that *starts with* student curiosity. 💡

CHAPTER SIX

Reengineering Learning with Curiosity in Mind

Over the past few years, I've stood in front of educator audiences in many locations and posed the following riddle to them: What single factor drives the following positive outcomes?

◊ It's as important as intelligence in student achievement.

◊ It supports better job performance.

◊ It leads to better relationships.

◊ People with more of it have greater life satisfaction.

◊ It helps us live longer.

◊ It predicts leadership ability.

Rarely, if ever, do audiences arrive at the correct answer immediately. Usually, they cast about for a minute or two, offering responses like, *Persistence? Grit? Motivation? Gratitude?* When someone finally offers the right answer—*curiosity*—the crowd emits a drawn out *ahhh* of recognition. *Why, yes, of course. Curiosity.*

The farthest thing from our minds

These interactions are not so different from what researchers find when they survey teachers. When asked to list important outcomes of learning off the tops of their heads, rarely, if ever, do teachers volunteer the concept of *curiosity*. Yet when they see it on a list, they give it high marks for something they hope to cultivate in students.[1] In short, teachers aren't *opposed* to curiosity; it's just been the farthest thing from their minds.

And who can blame them? As the previous chapter noted, public school teachers' performance assessments (and even pay) have increasingly been based on how well their students perform on high-stakes tests. In this pressure cooker environment, who has the time to think about curiosity, let alone cultivate it? Thus, we appear to have perfectly engineered our education system to produce the results of student disengagement and waning curiosity the longer they stay in school.

Schooling with curiosity in mind

So, what would it look like if we were to reengineer our schools and classrooms to produce different outcomes—namely, increased motivation and curiosity? What if instead of applying the dismal science of economics to schools to pressure them to improve, we applied positive psychology to create a system of schools and classrooms that tap the innate power of student curiosity?

If that sounds like a bridge too far, it's really not. Already, a great many teachers *do* unleash student curiosity in their classrooms. Mihaly Csikszentmihalyi and his colleagues, in fact, found this in their study of teenagers; while most classrooms were tedious environments, a few stood out as vibrant examples of engagement. In these classrooms, teachers sparked and maintained students' interest by modeling passion and enthusiasm for their subject areas, which sent a message to students that mathematics, art, or literature were full of fascinating and useful ideas and worthy of long-term pursuit. They also helped their students connect what they were learning to their own interests, lives, and long-term goals. One such insightful teacher, for example, launched a student's interest in a fashion design career when she told her student that, as a nonconformist, she might enjoy reading about another iconoclast: Coco Chanel.

Good teachers have always done this—taken the time to cultivate student curiosity and interest in what they're learning, just as my daughter's 2nd-grade teacher did for her with an overnight science experiment that made her excited to go to school on a snowy morning. Interestingly, her teacher was a bit of an iconoclast himself. Years earlier, he'd helped to start a district-sponsored magnet school in which parents and teachers had come together to create an alternative approach to schooling, one that would focus on "sparking the intellectual curiosity of our students." Later, he found his way to our neighborhood public school, and Molly found herself in his class. It's likely no coincidence that while in his class, she not only experienced regular doses of curiosity, but also began to appreciate curiosity as an admirable trait in herself and others. (For example, on Veterans Day, she proclaimed that veterans are "brave and always curious," which in her estimation was apparently the highest possible compliment anyone could receive.)

Years ago, at the advent of the standards-based education movement, a colleague and I facilitated focus groups of parents from across the U.S. to glean their opinions on public education as well as the need for standards, testing, and accountability to improve educational outcomes.[2] While listening to parents express their hopes and dreams for their children and what they wanted from their schools, it became clear that proficiency on standardized achievement tests was, at best, of marginal concern to them. Sure, they wanted to know that their students could read, write, and do math, but mostly they wanted their kids to be in schools where they were safe, respected, and able to flourish—to develop their own unique talents, abilities, and potential as human beings.

I emerged from those sessions wondering if the time, energy, and expense poured into concocting a dizzyingly complex system of measures, sanctions, and rewards in the name of reform had been worth it, especially when the results these systems were designed to create were largely deemed inconsequential for most parents and students. I returned to those thoughts on that snowy winter morning, when I realized that—complex school rating systems notwithstanding—my brief interaction with my daughter as she bounded down the stairs to breakfast spoke volumes about her school: She loves learning so much she hopes it's *not* a snow day.

I also found myself wondering, *What if that could be true for her every day?* And on a larger scale, could be true for *every* student every day? In other words, what if back in 2001 we had proclaimed that instead of leaving no child *behind*, we would seek to leave no child *incurious*? That may sound fanciful . . . but if we set curiosity as an aspirational goal, and wonder together how we might help kids become and stay curious, we may see that it's not so far-fetched after all, but well within our reach.

Designing curious classrooms

In her book, *The Fires in the Mind*, Kathleen Cushman[3] poses a thought-provoking question to several teenagers: What does it take to get good—really good—at something? After dozens of interviews, she concludes that *all students* have a passion to learn *something*—to dig more deeply, explore, and learn about something of interest to them. In short, they're all naturally curious about something. Under the right conditions (which may include support from adults or, alternatively, adults staying out of the way), they're apt to fan an initial spark of interest into a flame of ongoing interest and, ultimately, a fire inside to become a lifelong learner.

These right conditions for curiosity reflect, in many ways, the "unschooled" childhoods of Eleanor Roosevelt, Martin Luther King, Jr., Winston Churchill, Mahatma Gandhi, Theodore Roosevelt, and other great figures in history that Mildred Goertzel studied with her husband and son. In short, when it comes to unleashing kids' curiosity, there's no specific formula, checklist or program (30 Days to More Curious Kids!) to follow. Rather, we must focus on creating the *right conditions* for curiosity to flourish by keeping in mind a few important principles that emerge from research on student motivation and curiosity.

Curiosity Principle #1: Embrace not knowing.

Kids are more curious when they know that it's *OK to not know something*—that is, to have a gap in their knowledge. Recall what Mary Ainsworth discovered about children whose mothers provided them with "safe harbors" for exploration: Curiosity involves an element of risk taking. We must delve into an area we know little about or where we feel incompetent. And we're more likely to do that when we feel safe to admit we *don't* know something. Thus, we need to help our kids see that it's *OK* to profess *ignorance*, yet a *shame* to profess *indifference*. We can do that by saying things like, "I LOVE that question because it shows you're thinking deeply about this. How would you find an answer to it? When you do, let me know what you learn because I'm curious about it, too."

Curiosity Principle #2: Ask fewer, but deeper questions.

A thoughtful question or two can pique curiosity, but a bunch of them does not. As obvious as that sounds, the latter approach—

Curiosity-provoking and -sustaining questions

"Different-lens" questions ask students to view their learning from a different perspective. For example, shifting a conversation about science to one about ethics, economics, society, philosophy or the like. (Would it be right to use genetic engineering to bring the wooly mammoth back to life? Can scientific thinking make you happier?)

"Mash-up" questions ask students to consider two seemingly unrelated ideas or apply what they've just learned in a completely novel context. (Imagine a comic book hero whose superpower is the ability to breathe like an earthworm—in what situations would that be helpful? How is *Lord of the Flies* similar or dissimilar to *The Hunger Games*?)

"Non-questions," a term coined by University of Melbourne professor John Munro, who studies gifted and special needs learners, don't ask a question at all, but rather, prompt students to reflect upon, explain, analyze, or offer an opinion about what they're learning.[5] (Describe the psychological and societal implications of most maps being drawn with north on top and out-of-scale depictions of land masses at higher latitudes. Describe some ways you think people can be controlled by fate and other ways they can operate with free will. Write and solve a word problem that applies the quadratic formula to a real-life situation.)

peppering students with questions—appears to be common in education settings. A study of 18 college classes, for example, found that nearly 80 percent of the questions asked during a lecture were low-level recall questions. Twenty-three percent of them, in fact, required a simple yes or no answer. And, the more questions the professors asked, the less complex their questions were.[4] In contrast, the professors who asked a few thoughtful questions at critical junctures engaged students in much deeper levels of thinking, which suggests that asking kids to recall what they already know will do little to spark their curiosity, whereas encouraging them to build on what they know by surfacing new questions or knowledge gaps sustains their curiosity. For parents, this suggests we might want to replace the tired question, "What did you learn in school today?" with more engaging and thought-provoking questions, like, "When did you experience joy today?" "What surprised you today?" "What are you wondering about now?" (see callout box on previous page for some additional deeper-thinking questions to ask kids.)

Curiosity Principle #3: Replace undirected questions with directed ones.

In *Ferris Bueller's Day Off*, Ben Stein parodies the consummate dull teacher by demonstrating a tried-and-true technique for boring kids to death—directing questions to no one in particular ("Anyone? . . . Anyone?") before answering his own questions (". . . the Laffer curve"). Studies have shown that in most classrooms, a handful of students dominate the conversations, following something close to an 80/20 rule: 20 percent of students do 80 percent of the interacting with teachers.[6] That means the other 80 percent of students may be doing little to think deeply or to feel any sort of curiosity about what they're learning. To keep students engaged, teachers need to replace undirected questions (posing a question to the entire class and waiting for voluntary answers) with directed questions (thoughtfully calling on individual students to answer questions).[7] One such approach, called *numbered heads together*, groups students in teams of four to consider a response to a teacher question before calling on individuals (by number) to respond. It has been found to virtually eliminate student failure on subsequent content tests.[8]

Curiosity Principle #4: Use questions to provoke thought and analysis, rather than to simply elicit correct answers.

As noted earlier, sustained curiosity requires an element of courage— admitting we don't know about something while feeling confident we can find the answer. Sadly, studies have found that kids who struggle to learn often lack this courage and confidence, and thus tend to avoid interacting with teachers out of fear of embarrassment.[9] Moreover, to further protect their self-esteem, they tend to disengage from learning, telling themselves it's not important. Quizzing kids to see who knows the answer can exacerbate many students' existing anxieties and disengagement. It's not surprising, then, that research finds that as whole-group instruction (an intimidating environment for low achievers) increases in middle school, high-achieving students participate more in lessons and low-achieving students participate less.[10] However, in classrooms where teachers use questions to pique students' deep thinking and curiosity, and carefully consider student responses instead of quickly sizing them up for accuracy, low-achieving students (and all students for that matter) become more engaged.

Curiosity Principle #5: . . . Wait for it.

Perhaps the most important thing adults can do to encourage kids' curiosity is something we've known for decades—ever since it emerged, somewhat accidentally, while researcher Mary Budd Rowe sat listening to hours of audio recordings of classrooms to evaluate the effects of a science curriculum on student dialogue. While transcribing the conversations, she detected an interesting pattern. In most classrooms, teachers peppered students with questions, and students responded quickly with short, clipped answers. Yet in three classrooms, teachers let a long pause hang in the air after asking a question; after a few seconds, students responded with slow and deliberate answers, taking time to gather their thoughts. When Rowe began using a stopwatch to measure the pauses (which she called "wait time"), she found if they extended for three or more seconds and if teachers avoided cutting off students' responses, students were less apt to say, "I don't know," and more likely to support their responses with evidence. Students' responses were *three to seven times* longer than those of students in short-wait-time classrooms. Longer wait time also prompted more questions *from students*. In short, students demonstrated greater curiosity.

Curiosity Principle #6: Let students follow their curiosity.

Because curiosity is personal—what one person finds interesting, another may not—we cannot *force* kids to be curious about a particular topic; rather, we need to give them some latitude to explore ideas and find their own interests in what they're learning. Even small choices in learning (what essay topic to write about, or how to demonstrate their learning) have been shown to increase kids' motivation, performance, and willingness to take on challenging learning tasks[11]—a pattern similar to the childhood experiences of great figures in history who loved learning yet often hated school, and thus did much of their learning beyond the classroom walls while guided by nurturing mentors and tutors. Theodore Roosevelt, for example, whose mother and governess taught him at home, would scour the nearby woods for dead specimens of mice, snakes, and birds to examine.[12] At school, Albert Einstein raced ahead of other students, teaching himself geometry and algebra and deriving his own method for proving the Pythagorean theorem.[13] At home, family friend and tutor Max Talmud encouraged young Albert's interests in mathematics, philosophy, and science. In short, curiosity is more likely to flourish when kids are free to pursue their own interests alongside supportive adults who offer well-timed nudges to guide their exploration and keep their curiosity alive.

Curiosity Principle #7: Go play outdoors.

Nationwide, a growing number of preschool and early childhood programs are encouraging kids to go outside and play; in the past six years alone, the number of early childhood centers embracing learning in natural environments has increased five-fold.[14] Many of these programs were inspired by Richard Louv's book *Last Child in the Woods*, which links increases in childhood problems like obesity, depression, and attention deficits to kids spending more time indoors (often interacting with media and technology), creating what Louv dubbed "nature-deficit disorder."[15] Some studies suggest the best medicine for hyperactive or depressed kids may simply be a healthy dose of sunshine, fresh air, and unstructured playtime. For example, one study of 96 parents whose children had been diagnosed with attention deficit disorder found that these children were far less hyperactive after interacting with nature (for example, going fishing) than after spending time indoors (for example, playing video games).[16] And a study of 70 six- and seven-year-olds observed that after controlling for other factors such as verbal ability, age, and household income, children who spent more time in *unstructured*, self-directed activities (playing with friends, camping, drawing, visiting libraries, reading) demonstrated greater ability to engage in self-directed thinking than those who spent more time in *structured*, adult-directed activities, like organized sports, music lessons, or homework.[17] These findings left the researchers wondering if a 50-year shift in how kids spend their time—away from less structured, self-led activities, like sandlot baseball and fishing in the creek, and toward structured, adult-led activities, like organized sports—may be impeding kids' ability to persist in self-directed learning, a critical component of curiosity.

A new crossroads

To be clear, these seven design principles for curiosity aren't meant to suggest that children need *no* structure in their lives. To the contrary, when it comes to creating conditions for curiosity to flourish, we need to provide a balance between guidance and support from adults with freedom and latitude for learning—a happy medium that I observed one sunny day in April not too long ago, when I found myself standing on a pool deck at Aptos High School in the hills above Monterey Bay in California.

All around the pool were droves of teenagers sporting lab coats, suits, and other "uniforms" to represent their teams in a regional underwater robotics competition. As I watched the teens feverishly readying their robots to be immersed underwater to engage in simulated "missions" based on real-life challenges that confront the U.S. Coast Guard and other maritime agencies, I realized what was perhaps most remarkable about the entire scene: It was a *Saturday*; no one *had* to be there. Yet the teens were all visibly pouring themselves into the task, reviewing notes taken from a 400-page, college-level textbook and perfecting their "sales pitches" for engineers from a nearby oceanographic institute, called in to judge the competition and "buy" the best robot.

In many ways, the whole experience demonstrated a perfect balance between adult guidance and student self-organization—a balance that sadly seems to have been overlooked in how schools across the U.S. have responded to the latest "crisis" in education: the imminent threat of not having enough kids interested in science, technology, engineering, and mathematics (STEM, for short).

This latest call for school reform was sparked, in part, by *The New York Times* columnist Thomas Friedman, who returned from his travels in a competitive, crowded, and climate-change-ravaged world so convinced that the U.S. is falling behind in the race to equip our students for the jobs of the future that he warned his daughters, "Finish your homework—people in China and India are starving for your jobs."[18] Dire warnings from Friedman and others, combined with test score data that seemed to show U.S. students falling further behind their international peers in math and science, led business groups to sound the alarm about a "skills gap" in STEM fields, where they project a shortfall of 5 million workers by 2020. Not everyone is convinced of these projections; some skeptics, like political scientist Andrew Hacker, insist it's yet another manufactured crisis, driven by business interests seeking to keep the number of guest-worker visas high so they can keep wages low.[19] Others question whether pushing STEM on U.S. kids is warranted given that many countries that seemingly outperform the U.S. in math and science place little or no emphasis on STEM.

Nonetheless, if we accept that our students are apt to find themselves in a rapidly changing, increasingly competitive, high-tech world with no shortage of complex challenges, we might ask ourselves: How can we help them master the knowledge and skills they'll need to survive in this uncertain future? One response would be to do more of what we've been doing: enrolling kids in STEM schools and programs. In theory, such programs and schools are supposed to get more students interested in and ready to pursue careers in STEM. Yet in practice, that's not what's happening. Few kids who enroll in these schools emerge more interested in pursuing STEM careers than when they entered. For example, a study of 1,250 students in selective STEM schools found that students who entered these schools with only mild interest in STEM emerged no more likely to pursue STEM-related college coursework or careers.[20]

As a panel commissioned by the National Research Council to review research on STEM schools concluded, these programs did little to develop students' interest or curiosity in these fields.[21] That's likely because, according to the panel, getting kids interested in STEM hinges on providing them with rich "research experiences in high school," including "scientific investigations and engineering design projects."[22] To spark student interest in STEM, the panel noted, kids need to grapple with big ideas and "fundamental questions" about the natural world, so they learn to think like scientists. "However," the panel concluded, "this type of STEM instruction remains the exception in U.S. schools"[23] because all too often, our current assessment and accountability schemes, which rely heavily on multiple-choice items, limit the "content and complexity of what [states] test."[24] In other words, instead of helping kids think like scientists, many STEM programs fixate on helping them think like test-takers. For example, a study of 51 STEM academies in Texas found that while they trumpeted their ability to promote inquiry and project-based learning, in reality, most relied heavily on didactic instruction and explicit test preparation.[25]

A path less traveled

It doesn't have to be this way, of course. We could choose a different path—one that focuses on engaging young people's *curiosity* in science, technology, engineering, and mathematics (and other subjects, for that matter) by taking a problem-solving approach akin to what students encounter in elite colleges like Massachusetts Institute of Technology (MIT). In fact, in urban and high-tech enclaves across the U.S., a new generation of extracurricular math programs and competitions are cropping up that are producing world-class high school mathematicians and showing that kids of all backgrounds can master rigorous learning when adults challenge them with open-ended, multifaceted problems that students must apply deep learning to solve.[26]

Such an approach reflects not only the design principles of curiosity-driven learning described earlier in this chapter, but also what I saw at the underwater robotics competition in California. In many ways, the magic of this experience was that it gave kids the opportunity to see, touch, and feel what they were learning and apply big science ideas like buoyancy, water displacement, and electricity when designing their robots. The teens also brought their own personal interests to self-organized "companies" they had created to design, build, and sell the robots, assuming titles like marketing director, project manager, science officer, engineer, chief financial officer, and CEO.

Adults were visible around the school and pool deck that day, serving as mentors, coaches, and judges. Yet they weren't lecturing, quizzing, or demanding. Rather, they were simply nudging kids forward, fueling their curiosity. Nonetheless, the lessons the kids were learning were deep, complex, and motivating; I heard more than a few students express being starstruck in the company of engineers and scientists from Woods Hole Oceanographic Institute, where they hoped to work someday. In short, this "un-school" competition appeared to do what many STEM schools do not: get kids interested in STEM learning.

At this point in the book, I could sound the alarm that the lack of student curiosity in our schools is nearing crisis proportions, and if we don't solve it, other countries are going to "out-curious" us and leave our children leading meager lives of toil, trouble, and tedium. But I'm not going to do that.

For starters, we've seen that our schools have been afflicted with too many crises as it is—often with the implication that educators and schools are to blame for (or perhaps the only way to fix) yet another societal shortcoming. That's not very inspiring. Nor is it productive. As we'll see in a subsequent chapter, trying to frighten people into action is usually counterproductive. Moreover, curiosity doesn't work like that. We don't become curious because someone forces or frightens us into a state of curiosity; rather, we experience it because deep down, we *want* to be curious and find joy in exploring, investigating, and discovering something new.

So, rather than using the rhetoric of crisis and urgency to send schools and educators frantically scrambling to make kids curious, measuring student curiosity *ad nauseam* and fretting about kids who we just can't seem to make curious, let's come to the challenge of helping our kids be curious with a sense of optimism, hope, and wonder, considering what might be possible if we were to redirect our focus and energies toward creating places where kids can be curious. Let's imagine together how captivating and powerful it would be for our schools, classrooms, and kids' lives to be filled with curiosity— for our kids to pump their fists on a snowy morning because it's still a school day or to feel there's no better place to be on a Saturday than back at school for an underwater robotics competition. If we could do that—give our kids the gift of curiosity—not only would it likely make learning easier, deeper, and more joyful, but also, as we'll see in the rest of this book, it could make a great many other things about our lives and futures better, starting with the places where, as adults, we spend much of our time: at work.

PART III

Curiosity At Work

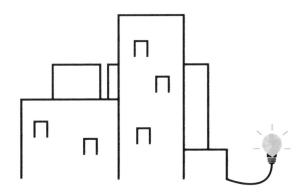

"Around here, we don't look backwards for very long. We keep moving forward, opening up new doors and doing new things, because we're curious ... and curiosity keeps leading us down new paths."

–Walt Disney

CHAPTER SEVEN

When Companies Lose Their Curiosity

In the early 1990s, Motorola was the unrivaled leader of the handheld phone industry, dominating 30 percent of the global market for cell phones. It had just launched a new product, the StarTac, which was, by all accounts, an engineering marvel—the most compact phone ever invented. The clamshell design fit nicely into the front pocket of a pair of pants and promised to put an end to embarrassing "butt dialing." Yet, as history would show, even as Motorola reached the heady heights of this crowning achievement, its downfall had already begun.

At first, no one inside Motorola headquarters in Chicago paid much attention to the emerging threat—the advent of new digital cell phones. The "smart money" inside Motorola said digital systems would require multi-billion-dollar investments in infrastructure that U.S. carriers, like Sprint and Verizon, were still loath to make. Moreover, carriers in the U.S. could not agree on a uniform operating system, so anyone foolish enough to buy a digital phone would find that a phone that worked in one locale wouldn't work in another. Who would want that?

So, Motorola stayed the course and kept cranking out analog phones. And why not? They were the big fish in the pond with no rivals . . . no *serious* ones, anyway. Sure, they knew that European carriers had agreed to upgrade their systems to support digital phones and that up in frozen Finland, a company called Nokia had announced it would begin developing digital phone technologies, an announcement met with scorn at Motorola headquarters. Nokia? How is that even pronounced? Besides, the Finnish company was best known for making rubber boots for fishermen and had just gone through a tumultuous upheaval with the suicide of its previous CEO. It was now being run by a new CEO who hadn't come from the fast-paced world of technology, but rather, the staid, buttoned-up world of banking. A banker! The top brass at Motorola smugly assured each other that their market dominance would continue well into the foreseeable future.

Then, a funny thing happened: Nokia's digital phones started to catch on—a trickle at first, then a steady stream, and eventually a torrent of sales. Its revenues quadrupled from $2.1 billion in 1993 to $8.7 billion in 1997. Soon, all of Europe adopted a digital standard for cellphones. By 1998, Nokia had gone from being nonexistent in the cellphone market to its number one player.

How did Motorola respond? It chose to counter the threat by doubling down on its investment in analog phones.

What?! The head-scratching logic inside the Motorola headquarters was apparently this: *We're good at analog phones. We're successful making analog phones. Past performance will predict future results. We ought to stick to our knitting.* And stick to their knitting they did, while watching their global market share tumble by half.[1]

Blunders, blind spots, and bad fixes: Incuriosity at work

The executives at Motorola were all smart, talented people, yet as business researchers J. Stewart Black and Hal Gregersen have observed, they suffered from an affliction that's common to many groups—operating with a faulty mental map that prevented them from seeing, or taking to heart, the obvious. Motorola executives were hardly alone in having blind spots. At around the same time, a similar story unfolded at another long-admired blue-chip company. In 1996, Kodak released what it touted as a breakthrough camera, the Advantix Preview, a regular film camera with a digital viewfinder. Kodak touted their "breakthrough" camera as a way for users to see the picture they'd taken and decide whether to keep it on the roll before processing the film. The Advantix didn't take actual digital photos, mind you; it just offered a glimpse of what a photo would look like when printed.

Inside Kodak, the concept must have seemed brilliant; the company could enter the digital camera market while preserving its core business of selling film. Outside Kodak, most people regarded the Advantix as idiotic; few people wanted such a thing. As a result, Kodak's multimillion-dollar investment in the Advantix Preview flopped miserably, as Paul Carroll and Chunka Mui recount in their book *Billion Dollar Lessons*.[2]

From the outside looking in, Kodak's blunder seems obviously and profoundly shortsighted. They let their own internal need to sell film, and their discomfort with change, prevent them from seeing their product through their customers' eyes. As with the missteps at Motorola, outsiders might puzzle over how so many smart people could all have the same, huge blind spot when it comes to doing what businesses are supposed to do best: listen and respond to customer needs.

Seeing through blind spots is easier said than done, of course, even when data are staring us right in the face. Here's one more cautionary tale: Blockbuster Video. In 2004, it had 9,000 stores in 17 countries and millions of customers. It was awash in data, including customer surveys that said people *disliked* going to video stores and *hated* paying late fees. Moreover, they'd already seen the future of video rentals firsthand. A few years earlier, a Silicon Valley computer programmer, irate over paying a $40 late fee for the movie *Apollo 13*, hatched an idea for a new business—providing people with mail-order DVDs and no late fees, *ever*. While it was still a fledgling company, its founder, Reed Hastings, had offered to sell Netflix to Blockbuster, but Blockbuster had turned him down. So, Hastings shrugged off their lack of interest and grew his company. Meanwhile,

Blockbuster's customers left in droves and it spent the ensuing years shuttering one store after another until it went bankrupt in 2010, a mere six years after its peak.[3]

The executives at Blockbuster were also smart people with good information. However, like the executives at Motorola and Kodak, their own mindsets and blind spots got in the way. Many of the executives at Blockbuster had learned about business while working at retailers like Walmart and 7-Eleven, so they viewed the world through retailers' eyes and determined together that the best fix was the equivalent of selling more candy in the checkout aisle. They also faced a high-pressure environment with shareholders demanding quick results—which may explain why the CEO's bold proposal to drop late fees and invest heavily in a digital platform to rival Netflix's resulted in his fellow corporate officers, fearful of losing revenues, revolting and ousting him.[4]

Lazy brains and groupthink

Blunders, blind spots, and bad fixes are common among businesses, organizations, and groups in general. Frequently, when people come together, they do stupid things. That's likely due in no small part to how we tend to think about problems ... or just as often, prefer *not* to think about them. As cognitive scientist Daniel Kahneman explains it, our brains essentially have two operating systems—a *fast-thinking* brain, which operates quickly and automatically with little thought (it's what allows you to read the words in this sentence) and a *slow-thinking* brain, which requires attention and gets easily interrupted when our attention is diverted (it's what allows you to *comprehend* this sentence and read it critically).[5] Our slow-thinking brain is generally in charge, but it's lazy—in Kahneman's words, our brains are most "comfortable in low-effort mode."[6] Analyzing problems, peering around corners, considering other perspectives, surfacing and reexamining assumptions, and reflecting on what's working and what's not requires serious effort from our brains, which want to keep sliding back into low-effort mode.

Keeping our brains throttled up to high-effort mode seems to be even more difficult when we're in groups—due to what sociologist William Whyte long ago labeled *groupthink*.[7] Whyte observed a sort of inverse relationship between the number of people in a group and their ability to ask the right questions, make good decisions, and move forward with sound judgment. Somehow, two heads are not better than one. Often, the more heads in the mix, the worse the thinking. Whyte speculated that when we're in groups, we naturally want to fit in, so we seek to conform and to not rock the boat, even when we can see that our boat may be steaming toward an iceberg. Whyte observed groupthink in all walks of life—from companies where he saw obeisance and group harmony rewarded, to academia where he saw smart people grow reluctant to question the logic of mainstream thinking for fear of being ridiculed or drummed out of their profession.

When groups slide collectively into low-effort thinking, they're prone to a phenomenon that researchers at the Carnegie Foundation have coined *solutionitis* or "the propensity to jump quickly on a solution before fully understanding the exact problem to be solved."[8] Avoiding solutionitis requires digging deeper to understand the real nature of a problem. For example, when Proctor & Gamble wanted to develop a new product for mopping floors, instead of concluding they needed to create a better soap, its research-and-development team visited homes to observe real people washing their floors, which offered insights into the physical challenges of floor mopping that, in turn, led to the invention of the Swiffer.[9]

Creating collective curiosity

In his book *How the Mighty Fall*, Jim Collins recounts several cautionary tales of high-flying companies (including many he'd profiled in earlier books) that lost their way, fell into decline, and in a few cases went bankrupt.[10] Often what foreshadowed these companies' fall from greatness was an *increase* in unchallenged assumptions and a *decrease* in critical questions inside the organization. Take, for example, U.S. drug manufacturer Merck.

For more than 30 years, its president George Merck had insisted on putting patients ahead of profits. But in the 1990s, a new generation of leaders took over and focused the company on profits, which led to a frenzied search for a wonder drug, which executives hoped they'd found in a new pain reliever, Vioxx, even though numerous warning bells suggested otherwise. Clinical trials had shown Vioxx to be no more effective than aspirin, and, worse, it appeared to be causing dangerous side effects, including heart attacks and strokes. Yet no one at Merck seriously questioned the big investment in Vioxx; they assumed they were making sound, thoughtful decisions. When the bad news about Vioxx finally broke, Merck found itself mired in negative press, congressional hearings, nearly $1 billion in legal settlements, and a 40 percent (or $50 billion) drop in its stock valuation.[11]

For Collins, the dark chapter in Merck's history illustrates "hubris born of success" which is what happens when the rhetoric of success ("We're successful because we do these specific things") replaces penetrating understanding and insight ("We're successful because we understand why we do these specific things and under what conditions they would no longer work").[12] In short, low-effort thinking becomes more prevalent than high-effort thinking and companies begin to believe that their success lies in a particular product, a killer app, or the ways things have always been done. That hubris ("We're so great, we can do anything!") leads right into the next stage of decline, what Collins calls "undisciplined pursuit of more"—more growth, more profits, more acclaim—and eventually to a third stage, "denial of risk and peril," in which people explain away bad data, ignore warning flags, and quash dissenting opinions.

Successful companies and organizations, on the other hand, continually strive to understand the *underlying principles* of what makes them successful, and stick to those things. They demonstrate what Collins called "disciplined creativity" as they explore and test new ideas. They also resist the temptation to shift into low-effort thinking and groupthink by continually asking themselves *what* things are working, *why* they're working, and *under what conditions* they might no longer work. Basically, their success comes down to this: As individuals and as a group, they demonstrate sustained, *collective curiosity.*

So, how do they do it? As we'll see, it has a lot to do with the people they hire (they're curious), the people who lead them (also curious), and the conditions they create (to help everyone *stay* curious). The bottom line (literally) is that it pays to be curious—not only as individuals but also as entire companies. 💡

CHAPTER EIGHT

Inquire Within

On a back road in Wyoming, a rancher leaned against a fence post as he surveyed his flock of sheep, when a luxury SUV pulled up. Its window lowered and a man with an expensive suit, lacquered hair, and sunglasses leaned out and said, "Hey, I'll make you a bet."

"What's that, son?" asked the rancher, a blade of grass hanging from his lips.

"If I tell you the precise number of livestock in your herd, can I have one of them?"

The rancher considered the offer for a moment, shrugged, and replied, "Sure, give it a shot."

Gleefully, the man hopped out of the SUV, grabbed a laptop from the back seat, and flipped it open on the hood. He punched a few keys on the computer and a satellite image of the hillside appeared on the screen. After a few more keystrokes, the computer ran an algorithm and rendered a number.

"Nine hundred forty-two," the man announced.

"By gum, you're right," the rancher replied and gestured to his herd. "Go ahead. Grab one."

"Any one of them?"

"Yup. A deal's a deal."

The man bounded over the fence, grabbed an animal, and returned to his car with it.

"How about a wager in return?" asked the rancher. "I bet my whole herd against your car if I can guess your profession."

The city slicker smiled. "You got yourself a deal."

"You're a consultant," the rancher offered without hesitation.

The stranger's jaw dropped. "How did you know?"

"Well, you came here uninvited, told me what I already know, and showed you don't know a whit about my business. And now . . ." he pointed to the animal under the consultant's arm, "can I have my dog back?"

A consultant friend of mine shared that joke with me—a modern take on "greenhorn" humor, in which the rough-and-tumble realities of Western life cuts a know-it-all city slicker down to size. In greenhorn humor, we delight in seeing the city slicker get his comeuppance—not because he's naive, but rather, *incurious*—he doesn't know what he doesn't know *and* doesn't care to know it. It feels like karma when a condescending jerk gets put in his place. So, we might find it reassuring to know that something like karma appears to play out in the workplace, where fortune seems to smile on those who *know* what they don't know and are willing to learn.

When curiosity comes to work

We might start with this simple data point: Curious individuals appear to perform better on the job. A study of 233 service-industry workers, for example, found that those who reported greater curiosity by responding positively to such statements as "I want to know more" and "New situations capture my attention" were more willing to learn on the job, better able to connect with coworkers, and better able to adjust to new work environments. On top of that, it's likely no coincidence that these same workers also received higher on-the-job performance ratings from their supervisors.[1]

A similar pattern showed up in the automotive industry, where German researcher Patrick Mussel studied 320 entry-level workers in an automotive plant. First, he sized up their job-related curiosity with a survey (asking them to respond to such statements as "I am eager to learn" and "I carry on seeking information until I am able to understand complex issues"), then examined how supervisors rated those same employees on a variety of measures, including their ability to follow directions, work well with others, complete tasks independently, and work hard.[2] Across all these measures, Mussel found that curious employees received higher ratings from supervisors, were more conscientious, more open to feedback and direction, got along better with their coworkers, and had higher overall job performance. In fact, curiosity was even more predictive of job performance than a variety of other factors that employers more commonly use to screen new employees, including intelligence, social skills, customer-service orientation, conscientiousness, and agreeableness.

In a subsequent study, Mussel and his colleagues sought to determine if curious people might also be better suited for jobs that require creative thinking and innovation. The research team asked nearly 500 people working in 188 different job categories to take the same 10-question survey of job-related curiosity. Using an instrument developed at the U.S. Department of Labor, they also determined how much divergent thinking and/or innovation people needed to perform the essential duties of their jobs.[3] By cross tabulating these two data sets, they found a strong, positive link between curiosity and on-the-job innovation. In short, curious people were more likely to land (and perhaps stay in) jobs that required innovative or creative thinking.

Does it pay to be curious?

Given these data, we might wonder if it *pays* to be curious—that is, are curious people more likely to advance in their careers and earn higher incomes? Here again, the answer appears to be yes. Numerous studies have found, for example, that a handful of personality traits, including openness to experience, conscientiousness, and agreeableness—all of which are correlated with curiosity—are linked to higher incomes.[4] Moreover, when people are surveyed about their *coworkers'* curiosity, the consensus view appears to be that curious people are going places. A recent survey of more than 3,000 employees in China, Germany, and the U.S., for example, found that people felt their curious coworkers were more likely to:

◊ Seek out new experiences at work.

◊ Bring an idea to life at work.

◊ Have a unique talent at work.

◊ Have a lot of friends at work.

◊ Be promoted at work.

◊ Have a high salary.[5]

What's perhaps most interesting about this study is that only 20 percent of employees considered *themselves* curious. In other words, though they admired curiosity in others, they did not self-identify as curious (at least while on the job). Instead, they were more inclined to see themselves as *organized, collaborative,* and *detail-oriented*—admirable traits, to be sure, yet hardly fonts of innovation. Indeed, we might imagine that if such traits were the most prevalent in a whole group of people, they'd be more apt to suffer from the very sort of uncreative groupthink that spawned the creation of the Advantix at Kodak, clinging to analog smartphones at Motorola, ignoring the rise of mail-order DVDs at Blockbuster, or pushing the flawed drug Vioxx at Merck.

Another compelling data point to suggest that curious people draw higher salaries is this: Across several job categories, including many fields where average wages have remained stagnant, employers are quietly paying more for top talent, as evidenced by the rise in wages for the top 10 percent of workers in these fields.[6] For example, while pay remains flat overall for graphic designers, it has risen steadily for designers with web and mobile platform skills. The same pattern holds true for software programmers. In a global economy, the requirements of jobs may change so quickly that the real shortage may be, as economist James Bessen puts it, in "non-cognitive skills that allow people to excel at learning on the job."[7] In short, people who demonstrate a propensity to learn on the job—who know what they don't know and are curious enough to close their knowledge gaps—are more likely to constantly "retool" themselves, become more valuable to employers, and thus command a wage premium.

Curiosity thinking at work

Finally, it's worth considering the link between curiosity and critical thinking or the ability to engage in "high-effort mode" thinking— to analyze and evaluate data, reexamine opinions, and consider alternative viewpoints and courses of action. When surveyed, 343 executives of U.S. companies said the skill deemed most important for new hires was "critical thinking and problem-solving" (identified by 72 percent of executives). Following were collaboration and teamwork (63 percent), and communication (54 percent). [8] The skill *least* valued? Applied mathematics, believe it or not. In other words, employers aren't looking for people who merely score well on a math test (which, as you recall from previous chapters, is the focus of many STEM schools) but rather, people who can use that knowledge to work with others to solve complex problems (which is more akin to what kids do at an underwater robotics competition).

All of this might prompt us to ask a larger question: What happens if companies and organizations can fill themselves with whole teams of *curious* people? A two-year study of 28 companies by researchers at MIT's Sloan School of Management may provide an answer. It found that a company's "ideation rate"—that is, the number of employee-generated "winning ideas" that bubbled up to management for active development and implementation—was a key variable for predicting a company's growth and profitability.[9] Specifically, companies with more than 300 "winning ideas" per 1,000 active users (employees) over a two-year time frame saw their profits grow at a higher rate than those with fewer than 100 winning ideas.

Curiosity starts at the top

In many ways, curiosity appears to start at the top; the most innovative companies and organizations have leaders who are curious themselves. A study of more than 300 entrepreneurs found that those who demonstrated greater *entrepreneurial curiosity*—a penchant for mentally stepping *outside* their own companies to understand the broader competitive landscape so they could, in turn, challenge the status quo *inside* their own companies to ensure they were keeping up with competitors—tended to be more innovative, curious thinkers themselves. Most notably, they reported frequently coming up with "novel ideas" and employing "original thinking" on the job, while finding less satisfaction in simply mastering a skill or doing a job exactly how they learned it.[10] Perhaps not surprisingly, international executive search firm Egon Zehnder put curiosity at the top of its list of four key "hallmarks of leadership potential." From decades of studying effective executives, the firm found that the best leaders demonstrate "a penchant for seeking out new experiences, knowledge, and candid feedback and an openness to learning and change."[11] It advises clients to tease out potential leaders' curiosity by asking them interview questions like, "What do you do to broaden your thinking, experience, or personal development?" and "What steps do you take to seek out the unknown?" In short, when trying to find a great leader, they advise organizations to "look for those who have . . . an insatiable curiosity that propels them to explore new ideas and avenues."

Hiring curiosity

So, how do companies find curious employees? A first step might be to acknowledge that the usual process for screening talent—sitting down with them and asking questions to "get to know them"—is pretty worthless. A meta-analysis of 85 years of research found that the go-to screening tool for many companies—unstructured interviews—predict only about 14 percent of the variance in a prospective candidate's eventual job performance—a few notches above reference checks (7 percent) and years of experience (3 percent),[12] but still pretty dismal. According to this study, the best tool was a sample test—assessing a candidate's performance on a task they'd be asked to perform on the job—which predicted 29 percent of the variance in future job performance, followed by tests of cognitive ability (26 percent) and structured interviews (also 26 percent) in which candidates respond to consistent questions with their responses evaluated against criteria (often a rubric).

The only trouble is, most jobs wind up being more variable and complex than anything that can be measured through a test or structured interview. With that in mind, Jay Hardy, a researcher at Oregon State University, identified what he believes may be a better predictor of future job performance: curiosity. He studied the performance of 120 students in solving a complex task—in this case, a marketing problem that required both critical and creative thinking—and found that those with higher levels of curiosity, who expressed interest in "exploring unfamiliar topics and learning something new," performed better at this task. This prompted Hardy and his colleagues to advise companies to hire for curiosity and place curious people in roles that require creative and complex problem-solving.[13] Ostensibly at least, Hardy noted in a subsequent interview, that's what companies say they're looking for in new employees—their job postings insist they're looking for curious, creative people—yet, Hardy added, few companies actually hire for curiosity by asking questions or screening applicants based on their curiosity.[14]

How can companies hire—and retain—curious people? According to Kelsey Meyer, whose firm helps companies develop thought leaders and is thus on the lookout for curious employees at her clients' companies, one easy way to gauge curiosity is to simply ask people what they've been curious about over the past few months—what new skill or knowledge they've learned or taught themselves. She also recommends giving people a task before an interview to see how deeply they research the challenge or what fresh perspectives they bring to it. Finally, she tells employers to encourage candidates to bring their own questions to the interview. "Curious people will ask original questions—period," she writes. "If someone either has no questions or asks canned questions like, 'What do you like about your job?' it's a big red flag."[15]

Kristen Hamilton, cofounder of Koru, which provides training for first-time job seekers, said her company has isolated seven key traits that correlate with on-the-job performance. One trait, as you might have guessed, is curiosity; in fact, Hamilton views curiosity as the wellspring of many other positive characteristics, including empathy, creativity, innovation, and the ability to learn quickly. How does Koru find curiosity in its candidates? Hamilton asks candidates to share the last time they "geeked out" about something—the last time they really dug into something to learn its every nuance. "If someone doesn't have that quality," she says, "if they don't need to learn every single detail of the topic in front of them—they're probably not going to reflect that level of engagement in their work, either."[16] Finally, like Meyer, she invites—and listens carefully to— the questions candidates ask, as they reveal a lot about a person's curiosity or lack thereof.

So, do companies and organizations simply need to bring curious people together and let them work their magic? Well, not exactly. As we'll see in the next chapter, organizations and companies, like schools, can either suppress or supercharge curiosity depending on prevalence of one simple factor: the quantity and quality of the questions they ask. 💡

CHAPTER NINE

Creating Curious Organizations

Most companies and organizations engage in questioning and problem solving on a regular basis. They ask themselves what's going wrong and how to fix it. That's nothing new. They may also solicit employee feedback—conducting surveys or putting a suggestion box in the break room. Again, nothing new. They probably survey customers, too, asking them about their experiences, tastes, and needs. A recent survey of C-suite executives from 57 large companies (including IBM, GlaxoSmithKline, and Bank of America), in fact, found that nearly all of them (99 percent) rated creating a data-driven culture a high priority for their firms, yet only a third (32 percent) were having success building these cultures.[1]

What's getting in the way? The biggest obstacles cited included "cultural resistance to change" (32.5 percent), "understanding of data as an asset" (30.0 percent), and "insufficient organizational alignment and business agility" (25.0 percent). Nearly half of these executives worried, in fact, that the biggest threat to their firms related to their inability to use data effectively—whether it's responding nimbly to data (29.5 percent), harnessing data for competitive purposes (13.2 percent), or being outpaced by competitors more adept in data use (11.7 percent).[2]

In other words, companies are awash in data, yet they don't appear to be putting data to effective use—a seeming problem of "data, data everywhere and not a thought to think." It's likely these companies are all regularly looking at data and asking questions about their data. Moreover, as we've seen, people often make bad decisions even when all the relevant facts or data are right in front of them. Clearly, it's not simply having data or asking questions about it that makes the difference, but something else. So, what is it? As we'll see, it's largely the extent to which companies encourage people to feel curious about the data in front of them—asking better questions that lead to better insights, better actions, and better results. And how do they do that? Let's consider the following big ideas or, keeping in the spirit of wondering curiosity, *musings*.

Musing #1: Embrace mistake-ology.

One of the first reasons that people are often reluctant to embrace the use of data is that they fear a close examination of data will make them look bad, revealing weak sales, poor customer satisfaction, projects falling behind schedule—the list goes on and on. In short, people have little incentive to dig into data if doing so will only result in giving them a black eye.

From this we extract our first musing for creating curious organizations: Embrace mistake-ology. Yes, organizations and companies should strive for success and to deliver the very best possible results. But that's not always going to happen. Sometimes even the best laid plans fail. Also, people are human. They're bound to make mistakes. Embracing mistake-ology means studying our mistakes to avoid making errors—repeated mistakes. Leaders can set the tone for mistake-ology by admitting to their own mistakes—and even regularly celebrating them. "OK, so here's the biggest screw-up I made this month, and here's what I learned from it."

A study of the management styles of 142 CEOs of small businesses found, in fact, that companies whose CEOs created a so-called *promotion* focus, encouraging innovation and new ideas, had significantly higher performance than companies whose CEOs created a *prevention focus*, cautiously fixated on preventing errors. A *prevention* focus, the researchers concluded, may work in stable, predictable environments where doing business as usual delivers results. Yet it tends to be ill-suited to dynamic environments, where new ideas and rapid change are essential. In these environments, it's more important for leaders to create an open-minded *promotion* focus that encourages exploration and looking differently at problems, rather than a cautious *prevention* focus that puts everyone on high alert to avoid mistakes (and often results in people making more of them or hiding them).[3]

Musing #2: Focus on getting better, not being best.

Many leaders like to trumpet that their product/service/approach/ (fill in the blank) is the "best in the business." That might make for a good sales pitch, but if people inside an organization or company believe all that hype, it can mark the beginning of a company's downfall—going back to what Jim Collins refers to as "hubris born of success."[4] If we believe we're *great* when we're only *good* we'll never get *better*. Soon, an "if-it-ain't-broke-don't-fix-it" attitude begins to prevail and curiosity walks out the door.

By keeping the focus on getting better, leaders encourage curiosity. On one hand, this can include engaging in reflective practice to do what we know works even better or with greater precision—for example, mastering a sales pitch, perfecting the use of a drill press, or improving customer service. At the same time, a focus on getting better can also empower people to find or develop "everyday innovations" by, for example, making real-time adjustments to marketing materials, end cap displays, or software applications—something people are less apt to do if they're told things are fine exactly as they are, so don't mess with them.

Musing #3: Using data as a mirror.

In a larger sense, how companies approach data also reflects something of a Rorschach inkblot test of their collective mindsets.

Do they view data with an *internal* locus of control—that is, do they believe they can positively influence their outcomes and thus view data as feedback for improving processes, products, and strategies? Or do they view data with an *external* locus of control—chalking up disappointing data to market forces, customers just not "getting it," or unfair competition? Decades of research have found that individuals with a strong internal locus are generally more successful in life—for example, they graduate from college at higher rates than those with an external locus of control.[5] In business, a study of small companies found that those whose CEOs had a strong internal locus of control performed at significantly higher levels (including being less likely to go bankrupt) than those with CEOs who had an external locus of control.[6]

Likely, leaders' attitudes and dispositions can permeate an organization—for better or worse—and influence how everyone looks at data. For example, when we have an external locus of control, we're more apt to view data as a *window*—revealing more about *others* than ourselves (our customers are hard to please, our suppliers are letting us down, our competitors are unscrupulous). If, on the other hand, we have an internal locus of control, we tend to view data as a *mirror*, or a reflection of own practices. And only by reflecting on our practices, of course, can we hope to get any better.

All this likely goes a long way to explaining why so many companies struggle mightily to use data effectively: It's less a matter of processes or protocols and more a matter of personal psychology—namely, how people view the world. Ultimately, whether companies use data as a mirror or window comes down to the conditions leaders create for people to be collectively *curious* or collectively *incurious*, which, in turn, reflects what we know about the conditions that help curiosity flourish: We're more prone to feel curious when we feel safe to take chances, experiment and make mistakes.

Musing #4: Keep wondering what if . . .

Ultimately, better questions start at the top, with leaders communicating that questions are valued. That's important. The best bosses—those who encourage curiosity thinking among their direct reports and in their organizations—lead by asking questions, and lots of them. Warren Berger interviewed the CEOs of several successful companies and found they have a key trait in common: insatiable curiosity. In fact, many of these leaders disrupted entire industries with a powerful *what if* question—a question brimming with new possibilities:

◊ Square began with Jack Dorsey wondering *what if* his friend didn't need to lose a big sale to a customer simply because he couldn't accept a credit card payment?[7]

◊ Southwest Airlines similarly began with a guiding question: *What if* air travel were affordable for everyone?

◊ Apple disrupted the music industry by asking *what if* people could buy one song at a time?

What if questions are powerful because they help us to imagine better realities and open doors to new possibilities, rather than closing them. At times, they may seem wildly idealistic, reflecting a sort of childlike naïveté or wonder—what Berger calls a "beginner's mind" approach to old problems and stubborn challenges. Great leaders use their curiosity to keep everyone open to new possibilities—even small ones—that less curious leaders might overlook. Curious leaders, for example, see bright spots in data and, instead of dismissing them as a temporary blip or fluke, they become curious about them, often using them as stepping stones to build something even better.

For example, in the 1930s, the owner of a chain of successful restaurants in Washington, DC, noticed something odd while visiting one of his locations—customers were buying meals and snacks and stuffing them into their suitcases on their way to catch planes at nearby Hoover Airport. A less curious CEO might've dismissed the whole thing as an oddity, but he instead asked *what if* I approached an airline about providing passengers with box lunches to eat on the airplane?

The next day, he did exactly that, hammering out an arrangement with Eastern Air Transport. Within months, he'd expanded the service to American Airlines and 22 flights a day. Eventually, his bright orange trucks were delivering food to the tarmacs of 100 airports.[8] Unlike other companies that get hung up on selling particular products or services (Motorola clinging to analog phones comes to mind), the young entrepreneur saw his company's core business not as a particular product (root beer) or venue (restaurants), but rather, providing friendly service and making people feel special. Thus, he remained open to new possibilities—something he'd do again 20 years later, when he spotted a new way to serve people and make them feel special: opening a hotel in Arlington, Virginia, on which he affixed his name, JW Marriott.

Musing #5: Keep the us in curious.

Competition drives business, so it stands to reason that many companies and organizations want their employees to embrace competition. Yet too often, companies get this all wrong— pitting individuals, teams, or business units *inside* an organization against one another, competing for scarce resources—be it R&D investment, marketing dollars, or real estate on the home page. When this happens, innovation and organizational curiosity usually suffer. Microsoft, for one, learned this lesson the hard way when its "rank-and-yank" approach to performance appraisals led to a decade of stagnation by making employees loath to share ideas with one another for fear of elevating someone ahead of themselves. Years ago, I saw a similar crabs-in-a-can dynamic play out during a well-meaning organizational effort to foster innovation, which backfired because the same people voting to greenlight projects were also vying to fund their own projects with a limited pool of resources. As a result, no projects went forward, illustrating that when not wielded correctly, competition can thwart curiosity and creativity.

An interesting paradox emerged in MIT's study of innovative companies shared in the previous chapter. The most innovative companies were able to harness the power of competition to extract *and share* the best ideas from their employees. They did so by creating "marketplaces" for employees to offer suggestions for improving performance, and in turn created structures and processes to encourage the best ideas to go viral. For example, at a chain of health clinics, an employee devised a clever solution for helping patients on restricted fluid intake stay hydrated during a time-consuming therapy that could leave them feeling parched—printing tips for managing fluid intake on the side of a spray bottle. Unlike in other companies, where employees might feel compelled to keep their good ideas under wraps—at least until the CEO showed up for a visit—this simple but effective innovation quickly spread across the other clinics, which readily adopted it.

How did that happen? As it turns out, quite by design. Over the years, the chain of clinics had developed formal programs to encourage and share innovation, including leaders regularly touring facilities for better ideas in "innovation road shows" and actively seeking ideas in March Madness-style "brackets" that encouraged curiosity thinking and allowed the best ideas to rise to the surface and get shared across the entire company. For workers in the clinics, these programs not only showed management was serious about innovation, but also fostered some friendly competition to create "winning ideas," which ultimately became everyone's idea when shared across the company. At my own organization, we try to foster the same ethos by purging certain phrases from our lexicon, including "my research," "my slides," "my presentation," and "my client," in favor of "our slides," "our presentation," and "our clients."

Musing #6: Encourage "revolving door" thinking.

In 1985, Andy Grove, then president of Intel, faced a difficult decision: whether to abandon what had once been his company's bread-and-butter product line, memory chips. Japanese manufacturers had begun to cut deeply into Intel's market share with lower-priced products. Meanwhile, Intel had made a breakthrough with a different product: microprocessors, which it was selling to IBM to use in personal computers. The question before Intel was straightforward, but agonizing: Should they abandon memory chips and focus on memory processors? Abandoning a declining core business would be heart-wrenching, requiring the layoffs of 7,000 people, nearly a third of Intel's workforce. Yet clinging to a failing product could sink the entire company and cause them to miss out on what, increasingly, was looking like the future of the business.

Basically, Grove found himself confronting the very same burn-the-ships question that many other leaders—including those at Motorola, Kodak, and Blockbuster—had faced, yet ultimately lacked the courage, insight, or curiosity to follow to its logical conclusion. After long hours of agonizing, Grove had an inspiration. As he recounts in his memoir, *Only the Paranoid Survive,* he turned to Gordon Moore, with whom he ran the company, and asked,

> "If we got kicked out and the board brought in a new CEO, what do you think he would do?" Gordon answered without hesitation, "He would get us out of memories [memory chips]." I stared at him, numb, then said, "Why shouldn't you and I walk out the door, come back in, and do it ourselves?"[9]

With the clarity provided by the "revolving door test," Grove and Moore made the tough decision: They got out of the memory chip business. It proved to be an inspired choice. Abandoning the declining core business allowed Intel to focus on—and become the market leader of—the new market of microprocessors, thus securing the success of the business for many years to come. In a fast-changing world, though, sooner or later, all leaders must employ the "revolving door test," mentally stepping away from their businesses or organizations long enough to see the big picture with an outsider's (or even beginner's) perspective. Doing so reflects a whole different type of curiosity—a sort of "big picture" curiosity and willingness to "go meta"—to step outside our own businesses and organizations and see them as others do, to understand what's really happening around us and reexamine our assumptions, and to embrace tough questions even if they lead us to painful realizations or uncomfortable insights, like the fact that what's worked for us in the past will no longer work in the future—be it film developing, clamshell analog phones, or video stores.

Leading with questions

Basically, what these musings add up to is that, contrary to the popular perception that leaders must have all the right answers, what's more important is that they ask the right *questions.* Leading through questions, though, can be difficult for many leaders because, as Berger notes, it requires a "rare blend of humility and confidence"—being humble enough to know they don't have all the answers yet confident enough to admit it to others. Such humble confidence is crucial for modeling curiosity thinking. It also reflects what Jim Collins refers to as a "Level 5 leader"—the kind of leader present in the most effective companies, one who has gotten past her or his own ego and "builds enduring greatness through a paradoxical blend of personal humility and professional will." In short, they keep driving their organizations to get better by continuously asking questions and engaging in their own continuous improvement; as Darwin Smith, CEO of Kimberly-Clark, whom Collins profiled, put it, "I never stopped trying to become qualified for the job."[10]

Quite likely, some business owners and organizational leaders may question the value of curiosity, worrying that asking (and permitting) too many questions may open a Pandora's box of people running around asking questions and challenging assumptions. Or they might think, *We already know what to do; we just need to do it.* They might assume they've already got a successful product, formula, or way of doing business; they just need to stay the course. Sometimes, they may be right . . . at least for a while.

Curiosity, though, isn't always a hammer for creative destruction. It can also guide our thinking in the other direction, helping us to "zoom in" to discover whether the core principles that made our company or organization successful in the first place will continue to make us successful (or help us be successful again) in the future.

By looking more deeply, we might see, for example, that our success was never about a particular product, offering, or activity, but rather, something more fundamental and replicable—perhaps the ability to understand and meet people's needs better than others, bring new products to market quicker than others, or build strong relationships with people and ensure their satisfaction. Such principles tend to be more timeless and grounded in what matters most, even as the outward trappings of what we do must continue to evolve in the face of changing customer needs, competitors, and technologies.

Opening new doors

Walt Disney seemed to understand all of this well. He never yoked his company to a single product—be it a movie, character, or even a place. Rather, he constantly reminded everyone around him that they were in business to do one thing: provide people with "magical moments." Even as they created blockbuster movies and developed popular amusement parks, they never gave in to hubris ("We're so great, we can do anything!") or came to believe they had figured out the single *right way* to make movies, create amusement parks, or deliver entertainment. Instead, they kept reinventing themselves, finding new ways to make people happy even as their customers, competitors, and technology kept changing.

And they never got stuck in the past, largely because as Disney himself observed, "Around here we don't look backwards for very long. We keep moving forward, opening up new doors and doing new things, because we're curious . . . and curiosity keeps leading us down new paths." Indeed, the ongoing "magic" of the Magic Kingdom appears to be that it bubbled out of an organization that consciously cultivated its own spirit of collective curiosity. 💡

PART IV

Curious at Heart

"You never really understand a person until you consider things from his point of view—until you climb into his skin and walk around in it."

– "Atticus Finch" in Harper Lee's novel, *To Kill a Mockingbird*

CHAPTER TEN

Alone Together

If we'd been alive at the turn of the last century, most of us would have lived in rural areas, where we would likely have interacted with only a few people every day. We'd talk to our family and maybe chat with a neighbor over the fence. On weekends, we might venture to town and converse with the local shopkeeper and fellow parishioners at our local place of worship—all people we likely would have known our whole lives. While few, our social interactions would have been deep, authentic, and self-regulated; in a small town or rural countryside, there would be no cloak of anonymity; we couldn't flip someone the bird from our horse carriage and not expect it to damage our standing in the community. Only occasionally might we interact with someone we *didn't* know: a stranger.

However, with the dawning of the industrial age and increasing urbanization of our society, all that began to change, as Susan Cain describes in her illuminating book, *Quiet: The Power of Introverts in a World That Can't Stop Talking.*[1] At the start of the 20th century, many people suddenly found themselves thrust into a world in which most of their social interactions were now with strangers. That created a great deal of anxiety for many—especially, as Cain argues, for anxious introverts who became avid consumers of a whole new industry of self-help books and seminars that aimed to help people develop more outgoing personalities, including the ability to be "fascinating," "magnetic," "forceful," "dominant," and "glowing"—a far cry from self-help books of the 19th century that encouraged "citizenship," "duty," "Golden deeds," "honor," "reputation," and "morals."[2]

Replacing interpersonal with impersonal

Nowadays, of course, most of us find nothing *strange* about interacting with *strangers*—they're all around us: at coffee shops, grocery stores, stop lights, and living in close proximity to us—maybe even in the same apartment building or down the block. In fact, for the overwhelming majority of Americans who now live in urban areas, we often find it *strange* to see a *familiar* face in a public place. As a result, the modern world, in Cain's view, has become an extrovert's paradise, a place where those who are adept at fist bumping and small talk thrive, while those prone to introspection, quiet conversation, and empathy may feel disquieted and overwhelmed.

Patricia Greenfield, a researcher at UCLA, documented a similar, dramatic shift in our culture by using the Google Books NGram Viewer to analyze the word choices used in thousands of texts published between 1800 and 2000—a period of time during which the U.S. population went from being predominantly rural (with 94 percent of Americans living in sparsely populated areas) to predominantly urban (with 79 percent living in densely populated areas).[3] The mosaic of words in print paints the picture of a culture moving away from communal obligation and toward individual self-determination: For instance, words like "choose" and "decide" increased five-fold while words like "duty" and "obliged" dropped to one-third of their previous levels; at the same time, "give" became less frequent while "get" became more prevalent, and words associated with *personal* emotion (e.g., "feel") eclipsed those associated with *interpersonal* action (e.g., "act," "deeds"). Greenfield also discovered a sharp decline in *other*-centered words, like "obedience," "authority," "belong," and "pray" and a pronounced rise in *self*-centered words like "individual," "ego," "personal," and "self."

Shortly after 3 a.m. on March 13, 1964, Kitty Genovese, a 28-year-old bar manager, returned home to her apartment in a two-story Tudor-style building in the Kew Gardens neighborhood of Queens. The street was enveloped in darkness as she parked her car 100 feet from the rear of the building, where stairs led to her second-floor apartment.

She halted when she spotted a man in the darkness, watching her. Frightened, she ran to the street in front of the building, hoping to reach a call box to alert the police. The man sprinted toward her, grabbing her arm as she ran beneath a streetlamp near a bookstore. She screamed. Lights went on in a nearby apartment building and a window slid open. Here, accounts of the story begin to diverge. According to the first retelling of the incident,[4] Kitty's cries for help echoed across the quiet neighborhood. "Oh, my God, he stabbed me!" she screamed. "Please help me! Please help."

"Let that girl alone!" a man called down from the window.

The killer released Kitty and walked away. But after the man in the upper window turned off his light, the attacker returned and caught Kitty as she crawled toward the safety of her apartment building, stabbing her again—this time, fatally. Afterward, the police said some 38 people had heard Kitty's cries for help, yet failed to confront her attacker, come to her aid, or alert the authorities. One told a newspaper reporter, "I didn't want to get involved."

Kitty's murder was just one of 636 in New York City that year, and as it turns out the circumstances of her death were sensationalized—in reality, only a half-dozen or so people heard her cries for help, not 38, and many did, in fact, call the police.[5] All those facts, however, did not fully emerge until years later, so at the time, the seeming indifference of her witnesses shocked a nation and brought about the creation of the 911 emergency system. Amid the outrage and soul searching, researchers began to delve into what causes people to turn a blind eye to the suffering of fellow humans. Soon, they coined a new term, *the bystander effect,* to explain the phenomenon of people in a crowd ignoring an individual's cries for help.

Sociologists began to wonder if the incident might reflect a darker malaise in the heart of our cities and national psyche—manifestations of what, decades earlier, Louis Wirth, a member of the renowned Chicago school of sociology, had labeled the "urban personality." A fundamental paradox of urban living, Wirth observed, is *being alone together.* City dwellers, he observed, live in "frequent close physical contact," yet are separated by "great social distance," leaving them feeling socially detached, giving "rise to loneliness." Because urbanites rub shoulders with more strangers than they can ever hope to relate to as individuals, they can grow increasingly detached and callous to one another's humanity. As a result, something inside slowly dies—something we might call empathy, compassion, or *interpersonal curiosity.*

All of this reflects, according to Greenfield, a massive sea change in our culture over the past 200 years: moving away from what German sociologists called *gemeinschaft* or *community*—mostly rural areas that relied on *interpersonal* dependence and placed a high value on duty, religion, and *group* welfare—and toward *gesellschaft*, or *society*— secularized urban areas where people interact mostly via *impersonal* commerce and place a high value on individual freedom and the accumulation of wealth—in short, the welfare of one's own *self.*

Looking for differences in indifference

In the years following Kitty Genovese's sensationalized murder, psychologists began to test the bystander effect on street corners across the U.S., the U.K., and Australia—curious if they might detect any differences in the helpfulness of people who live in small towns versus mid-sized cities or large urban areas. Usually, the experiments would go like this: A stranger standing on a street corner would make a simple request of passersby, like asking for directions or the time of day. At other times, they might make more serious requests, such as feigning injury and pleading for help. Over the course of dozens of studies, an interesting pattern emerged: People in larger communities (with 20,000-plus people) were generally more likely to assist their fellow human beings.[6] However, a later meta-analysis of 65 of these studies found what appeared to be a nonlinear curve: People in the smallest communities (less than 5,000) seemed to be most wary of, and reluctant to help, strangers. Helpfulness, in fact, generally rose with the population until places reached a threshold of 300,000 people—at which point, kindness toward strangers dropped significantly.[7]

Are we becoming less empathetic?

Following a similar line of inquiry, in 1979, researchers began surveying college students using a scientifically validated 28-item questionnaire designed to measure four different types of intellectual and emotional empathy:

◊ **Empathic concern** (e.g., "I often have tender, concerned feelings for people less fortunate than me.")

◊ **Perspective taking** (e.g., "I try to look at everybody's side of a disagreement before I make a decision.")

◊ **Fantasy** (e.g., "I really get involved with the feelings of the characters in a novel.")

◊ **Personal distress** (e.g., "When I see someone who badly needs help in an emergency, I go to pieces.")

The first two measures—empathic concern and perspective taking—are important because both have been strongly correlated with many positive outcomes: People who demonstrate *empathic concern* are less likely to demonstrate socially dysfunctional traits like boasting, verbal aggression, and loneliness. They're also more likely to volunteer, return incorrect change, let somebody cut ahead of them in line, carry a stranger's belongings, and donate money to charity. Similarly, people high in *perspective taking* are more likely to volunteer, donate to charity, and have high self-esteem, and they are less likely to demonstrate socially dysfunctional behaviors like boasting, verbal aggression, and loneliness. Moreover, schools where students rate high in both empathic concern and perspective taking have less bullying.

Conversely, people who rate low on empathic concern and perspective taking are more likely to demonstrate aggressive behavior while inebriated (read: They're "mean drunks") and to commit sexual offenses and child abuse, leading some researchers to conclude that these scales may be among the best available predictors of criminal behavior. The latter two measures—fantasy and personal distress—are both correlated with *antisocial* behaviors, including narcissism and avoiding others in distress.

Here's where we may have cause for concern: over the past three decades, these surveys (taken by more than 13,000 people) recorded a 48 percent decrease in empathic concern and a 34 percent drop in perspective taking. Stated differently, a majority of students in 2009 scored below the mean scores for perspective taking and empathic concern reported by students in 1979. (Meanwhile, the dysfunctional forms of empathy—*fantasy* and *personal distress*—remained unchanged).[8]

Although there's no scientific way to isolate the exact cause of these declines (it's impossible to subject entire generations to experimental studies), Sherry Turkle, a professor at MIT who has spent her career studying how people interact and communicate with one another, believes she may know a key reason—especially given that the sharpest declines in empathy occurred after 2000.[9] The answer, it seems, may lie in the revealing experiences of a handful of teenagers who voluntarily enrolled in a peculiar kind of detox program.

Looking for connections in all the wrong places?

For the teens in the detox program, going "cold turkey" spawned a wave of emotions—denial, resentment, and anger. Gradually though, through frank and sympathetic group conversations, they came to see that a habit that had started as a way to kill time and socialize had started to consume their lives, harm their friendships, and spawn abusive behavior and regrettable sexual decisions. Over time, as the cravings of their addiction lessened, they began to feel, as one student put it, "strangely happy."[10]

"It's cheered me up for some reason, I don't know why," a boy reported. "I feel different. I can concentrate more." By the end of a full week of detox, students had reengaged with their friends and found time to rekindle forgotten interests, like reading books. Unfortunately, when the program ended, most reverted to their old ways, which wasn't abusing drugs or alcohol, but rather, an unhealthy, habitual relationship with their smartphones. Nonetheless, their so-called "digital detox" had given them a new ability to set aside their devices without FOMO (Fear Of Missing Out).

These teens are part of a growing trend in which people voluntarily unplug from the internet and their smartphones for a few days to rebalance their digital and real lives. Cutting their ties to the web, many people find, makes them feel less frenetic and more content; by tamping down their digital cravings, they're able to attend to deeper longings, including fostering more meaningful ties with others. The experience of traveling back to a simpler time (of a mere decade ago), shows just how much smartphones and social media have changed our lives, likely rewired our brains, and altered how we interact with one another.

Recently, a national study of 20,000 Americans from health insurer Cigna found that loneliness has reached "epidemic" proportions in America, with nearly half of those surveyed reporting feeling sometimes or frequently lonely. Perhaps even more surprising, young adults (between 18 and 22) were the loneliest of any age group surveyed. Overall, on a scale of 20 to 80 (with 80 being most lonely) Americans' average loneliness was 44; young people's average score was 48, compared to an average of 39 for elderly Americans (over the age of 72).[11]

Consider that for a moment: At the very time when we imagine young people happily squeezed together in college dormitories, shared apartments, and crowded bars, they report *greater loneliness* than their grandparents' generation. Why should that be? Although heavy users of social media did not report being significantly lonelier than non-users, they didn't report feeling any *less* lonely, either. So, what's the best cure for loneliness? Not surprisingly, it's engaging in frequent, meaningful, face-to-face interactions with others. People who do this—engage in frequent, real-life interactions with other people—not only report less loneliness, but also better health outcomes.

As it turns out, loneliness is bad for your health. According to a meta-analysis of 148 studies involving more than 300,000 patients, the stress of chronic loneliness has the same negative effects on health outcomes as smoking 15 cigarettes a day.[12] What all of this may add up to is that as community ties have weakened and social media leaves us feeling, at best, like bystanders in other people's lives, we may all need to restore a different kind of curiosity in our lives— namely, curiosity about other people.

CHAPTER ELEVEN

The Curiosity Connection

Sherry Turkle, who has devoted her career to studying the impact technology has had on how we communicate, has found that even young people, who insist they're able to move deftly between the real and digital worlds, poignantly acknowledge that something's missing in their interpersonal connections, starting with their own parents' divided attention as they futz with phones at dinner, the park, or school events. Young people also report something missing in their real-life conversations with friends, which doesn't surprise Turkle, who can point to studies that show the mere presence of a phone on the table makes our conversations shallower; we tend to stick to lighter topics as we fear we'll get interrupted in the middle of heartfelt sharing. As a result, we're less likely to bare our souls, kick around big ideas, read others' emotions, or have the sorts of silences that provide openings to deeper issues, like our aspirations and values. When we "keep our phones in the landscape," Turkle observes, "we don't allow these conversations to happen."[1]

Restoring the lost art of quiet conversation

Moreover, says Turkle, "When we communicate on our digital devices, we learn different habits ... we start to expect faster answers. To get these, we ask one another simpler questions. We dumb down our communications, even on the most important matters." All of this tempts us, says Turkle, "to think that our little 'sips' of online connection add up to a big gulp of real conversation. But they don't."[2]

In fact, it seems that some kids' excessive use of screen time may be depriving them of an essential skill: the ability to read one another's facial expressions, emotions, and nonverbal cues. At least that's what we might glean from a study that invited 51 preteens to engage in a digital detox program by attending a five-day camp without their devices;[3] after less than a week, the preteens were better able than peers who had not attended the camp to infer emotional states from photographs of facial expressions and videos of people talking with the volume muted. So, while the bad news may be that digital devices can reduce our ability to read one another's emotions, the good news may be that we can restore it fairly quickly after just a few days of unplugging from our smartphones and plugging into one another.

Kentucky teacher Paul Barnwell discovered something similar when he spontaneously launched an unusual project with his high school class. After watching his students struggle to interview one another for an assignment, fumbling in their efforts to move beyond scripted questions and engage in spontaneous dialogue,[4] he asked his students to put down the smartphones they'd been using furtively under their desks and announced that their next project would be to "practice a skill they all desperately needed: holding a conversation."

After a long, bewildered pause, one student finally raised his hand. "How is this going to work?"

As his students gradually came to appreciate—and improve—their conversational skills, Barnwell realized "that conversational competence may be the most overlooked skill we fail to teach our kids." Indeed, "in our zealous rush to meet 21st century demands—emailing assignments, customizing projects for tablets and laptops, and allowing students to BYOD (Bring Your Own Device)—we aren't asking students to think and communicate in real time."

What these studies and observations may add up to is that, like the proverbial frogs in a boiling pot, our world has gradually—yet dramatically—changed around us in ways we've been slow to recognize. Like the tremendous changes at the turn of the 20th century, the turn of the 21st century has brought a whole new set of dramatic changes; increasingly, our world is filled with strangers and superficial interactions that have led it to morph into a hyper-frenetic *society* that our great-grandparents would scarcely recognize or know how to navigate. We've learned to cope with it by becoming bystanders in one another's lives, often substituting the occasional like or thumbs-up on social media for real human contact. Yet these connections often don't serve us well, as a recent review of dozens of studies comprising 35,000 people seems to suggest: Higher use of social media correlates with mental depression, especially if people spend much time at all comparing the selectively curated glimpses of other people's lives to their own.[5]

"Americans in the twenty-first century devote more technology to staying connected than any society in history, yet somehow the devices fail us: Studies show that we feel increasingly alone," write Harvard Medical School psychologists Jaqueline Olds and Richard Schwartz in the opening lines of their book, *The Lonely American: Drifting Apart in the 21st Century*.[6] Olds and Schwartz note that the number of people with whom Americans say they discuss "important matters" dropped from three to two confidants between 1985 and 2004; even more concerning (and reflective of the findings of the Cigna survey), the number who say they have *no one* with whom to discuss important matters *tripled* to one-quarter of all Americans. Perhaps not coincidentally, the number of one-person households has also increased steadily since 1940, rising from 7 to 25 percent by 2000. A recent survey found that nearly three-quarters (72 percent) of Americans report feeling lonely on occasion and fully one-third of Americans say they feel lonely once a week.[7]

In light of medical research showing that social connections help us to live longer, respond better to stress, and ward off illness, Olds and Schwartz (and others) note this epidemic of loneliness is also a health crisis. Moreover, they speculate that the rising number of adults and adolescents who use antidepressants may be related (at least in part) to the lack of meaningful interpersonal connections in their lives.

Becoming curious about one another

As we'll soon see, one possible antidote to loneliness, detachment, and declining empathy in our world of strangers may well be *curiosity*, albeit a more heartfelt version of curiosity that's less fixated on what other people *do* or *like*—their vacations, kids' activities, or reposts of news stories—and more intent on getting to something deeper, something that may have emerged more naturally in tight-knit *communities* where having fewer, deeper connections with those familiar to us may have provided something more meaningful than our smartphones could ever offer.

At this point, we might wonder: Can we really develop deeper connections with others? After all, don't relationships develop slowly (if not serendipitously) over a long period of time? Moreover, what could curiosity possibly have to do with intimacy?

It might be easy to chalk up intimacy and interpersonal connections to the vicissitudes of attraction and chance encounters—and to write off meaningful interpersonal relationships as enigmatic phenomena unrelated to curiosity—were it not for two research psychologists falling in love more than four decades ago and deciding to spend their lives researching this funny little thing called love.

Curious about love

As Arthur and Elaine Aron tell it, one kiss changed their lives. It was the summer of love, 1967. Both were students at the University of California, Berkeley, standing in front of Dwinelle Hall. "I fell in love very intensely," Arthur Aron recalls.[8] Rather serendipitously, he was also looking for a topic for his doctoral dissertation, so "just for fun I looked for the research on love, but there was almost none." So it was that the topic for his dissertation and, eventually, his life's work, came to him out of the blue, almost like a song.

In the coming years, he and Elaine would work together to apply scientific methods to study the secrets to not only romantic love, but also interpersonal closeness and intimacy. Over the years, they developed and refined a list of 36 questions and have asked thousands of randomly assigned pairs of strangers to respond to these increasingly intimate questions to see what effect they have on drawing people closer together. Although it wasn't the intent of the study, at least one pair of strangers got married six months after participating in the experiment,[9] which contributed to numerous reports that the 36 questions can lead to love—including a 2015 article in *The New York Times* that went viral in which Mindy Len Catron recounted how, on a lark, she and a casual acquaintance took the 36 questions out for a spin and wound up standing on a bridge at midnight, staring into each other's eyes and eventually (spoiler alert!) falling in love.[10]

36 questions to intimacy

So, what are these 36 questions, and what do they tell us about how to develop true interpersonal connections? Moreover, given that the experimental sessions were relatively brief—just 45 minutes, or about the time it takes for pizza delivery—how might we use them (or some portion of them) to restore the interpersonal connections that seem to have gotten lost in our superficial, frenetic, impersonal *society*? The 36 questions are grouped into three sets that foster increasingly intimate dialogue. The first set encourages participants to share their *preferences* and *interesting things* about themselves with one another with questions like these:

◊ Given the choice of anyone in the world, whom would you want as a dinner guest?

◊ Would you like to be famous? In what way?

◊ Take four minutes and tell your partner as much about your life story as possible.

The second set of questions encourages conversation pairs to share their *aspirations* and *values*, to reveal more *personal* information about themselves, and to begin to *talk about the other person in a positive way*, with questions like these:

◊ Is there something that you've dreamed of doing for a long time? Why haven't you done it?

◊ What do you value most in a friendship?

◊ How do you feel about your relationship with your mother?

◊ Alternate sharing something you consider a positive characteristic of your partner. Share a total of five items.

The third and final set of questions guides participants to become more *vulnerable* with one another, revealing *personal* and *emotional* information by responding to questions like these:

◊ Complete this sentence: "I wish I had someone with whom I could share . . ."

◊ Share with your partner an embarrassing moment in your life.

Participants also continue to share *what they like about* one another and find *shared connections* by responding to questions such as these:

◊ Make three true "we" statements each. For instance, "We are both in this room feeling . . ."

◊ Share a personal problem and ask your partner's advice on how he or she might handle it. Also, ask your partner to reflect back to you how you seem to be feeling about the problem you have chosen.

Together, the 36 questions compress into less than one hour what might normally take people weeks, months, or even years to share, moving them quickly from skimming the surface of their personalities (i.e., their *preferences*) to diving into their *values, aspirations, emotions,* and *regrets* before fostering *shared appreciation* and ultimately *mutual dependency* as they solve each other's problems. In many ways, the questions distill into a 45-minute conversation the essence of *community*—shared values, aspirations, and dependency.

Time and again, the Arons and their colleagues discovered that after just 45 minutes of sharing responses to these questions, partners reported a much higher sense of interpersonal closeness with one another than partners in control groups who engaged in unstructured small talk. Moreover, partners experienced the same effects regardless of whether they were paired randomly or intentionally based upon shared values or even *conflicting* values.[11] In other words, talking about values, aspirations, regrets, and challenges brought people of all stripes together, perhaps because it revealed there is more that unites than divides us.

It's also worth noting how different these brief yet intimate conversations are from our usual banter at backyard parties, chit chat when our smartphones are in the "landscape," or the unending stream of tweets, likes, and pins on social media. At best, such vehicles might lend themselves to sharing our *preferences* as we cheer on (or lament the travails of) our favorite sports teams, share about our vacations or children's latest feats, or comment on current events, but they do little to convey deep emotions or values, develop mutual dependency, or engage in shared problem-solving—the sort of values-based connections and interdependencies that were the fabric of smaller *communities* of yore and appear to be increasingly rare in our larger, more impersonal *societies*.

In a more recent study, Arthur Aron and a colleague asked 34 couples—17 in early-stage romantic love and 17 with 20-year-plus romances—to have their brains scanned while being shown photos of their partners as well as photos of "neutral" people (like their neighborhood dry cleaner). The scans revealed that when shown photos of their lovers, people's brains responded with high activity in their dopamine reward centers, releasing the same "euphoria" chemicals as satisfying hunger cravings, completing a task, or taking illicit drugs.[12] So, it seems that 80s pop star Robert Palmer may have had it right: We're addicted to love. Conversely, the brains of unhappy lovers did not register the same activity in their reward centers when shown photos of their partners, which suggests that when love fades, it does so in both our hearts and minds.

What does any of this have to do with curiosity? Quite a lot, as one of Arthur Aron's students discovered while digging deeper into the question of what makes love grow—and fade. 💡

CHAPTER TWELVE

Falling in Love with Curiosity

While working in Arthur Aron's research laboratory at Stony Brook University in New York, Todd Kashdan began to wonder what personality traits drive attraction in the first place. As with any set of data, the 36-question experiment produced variable results. Overall, the results were positive, but some conversation pairs formed even stronger bonds than others. Why should that be? Were some people more socially anxious than others, inhibiting their ability to develop strong bonds? Did some people listen better? Were some simply more positive, making them more likeable? Or could something else be at work . . . like *curiosity*?

Upon leaving Arthur Aron's lab for a position at the State University of New York at Buffalo, Kashdan began studying curiosity—exploring its links with such things as personal growth and goal attainment. Thinking back on his work with Arthur Aron, he wondered if curiosity might support *interpersonal connections*. Could curious people be better listeners, asking more follow-up questions and showing more interest in their conversation partners than incurious people? As no one had yet researched what role curiosity might play in forming interpersonal connections, Kashdan decided to follow his hunch and devised an experiment with his colleague, John Roberts.[1]

They invited 104 college students to engage in conversations with a stranger (in this case, a fellow student), following a simplified set of questions inspired by the Arons' 36 questions. Unbeknownst to the study participants, their conversation partners were confederates of Kashdan and Roberts; each confederate had been trained to provide consistently friendly yet neutral interactions during the conversations and report afterward on their experiences. Like the 36-questions experiment, the conversations began with small talk but soon become increasingly intimate, employing just five questions:

- ◊ If you could invite anyone, living or dead, for dinner and conversation, who would it be and why?
- ◊ Is there anything you find disturbing about immortality? If not, why not?
- ◊ If a crystal ball would tell you the truth about any one thing you wished to know concerning yourself, life, the future, or anything else, what would you want to know?
- ◊ Is there something that you've dreamed of doing for a long time? Why haven't you done it?
- ◊ When did you last cry in front of another person? By yourself?

Prior to the study, Kashdan and Roberts had measured participants on three scales:

1. Their general and current levels of social anxiety (how confident or fearful they felt in social situations).
2. Their positive and negative affect (for example, whether such conversations made them feel joyful and excited versus anxious and jittery).
3. Their levels of *trait* and *state* curiosity (how curious they felt in general and during the study itself).

Afterward, Kashdan and Roberts measured participants' interpersonal attraction and perceived closeness—the extent, for example, to which they believed they could "get along" or would "like to work together" with their conversation partners. (For good measure, they also assessed how well the study confederates had stuck to their scripts and interacted with participants in a consistently neutral manner). As a result, they now had several data points to compare using sophisticated statistical methods. Upon crunching the numbers, some surprises emerged.

First, participants with higher levels of *state* curiosity (and to a lesser extent, *trait* curiosity) reported feeling closer to their conversation partners afterward. Perhaps most strikingly, though, *so did their conversation partners*—who, recall, were confederates instructed to remain friendly yet consistently even-keeled with their conversation partners. Interestingly, positive affect had *no correlation* with interpersonal closeness for participants or confederates—that is, enjoying the conversations didn't help participants feel closer to their partners if their partners weren't also *curious* about them.

Turning small talk into dialogue

In subsequent experiments, Kashdan found that curious people appear to have a natural knack for turning small talk into deeper, more meaningful conversations. For example, he and a colleague invited participants (whom they had pre-tested and identified as having varying levels of *trait* curiosity) to engage in 45-minute conversations with strangers—with half of the conversations designed to be superficial banter, answering questions like "What is your favorite holiday? Why?" and the other half designed to be more intimate conversations based on questions like "When did you last cry in front of another person? By yourself?"[2]

Not surprisingly, all participants generally reported greater feelings of intimacy with their conversation partners after engaging in the intimate conversations compared with those who engaged in small talk. Yet some small-talk conversation pairs stood out as outliers, reporting feelings of closeness on par with those in engaged in the conversations structured for intimacy. What turned the small talk into more intimate conversation? As you might've guessed, at least one member of the pair was highly *curious*. From these findings we might extrapolate that when we're curious—and in the presence of curious people—even relatively brief *small-talk* conversations can turn into something more meaningful.

So, what exactly were curious people doing to turn small talk into meaningful conversations? For privacy reasons, Kashdan couldn't record or make transcripts of the private conversations, yet he found that people who were highly curious were also deemed by their conversation partners to be more open, tolerant, and energetic than non-curious people. Curious people appear to enter into dialogue with open minds and an eagerness to learn about someone else, which in turn encourages others to open up to them. That's the symbiosis between curiosity and intimacy; curious people delight in learning something new and their conversation partners delight in having someone understand them.

At first blush, that may seem like an asymmetrical sort of symbiosis— with one person satisfying an *intellectual* need (curiosity) and the other an *emotional* one (closeness). That hardly seems empathetic— after all, isn't the best way to connect with someone to assure them that we "feel their pain"?

Well, perhaps not.

The perils of feeling your pain

As it turns out, we human beings have an amazing capacity to *literally* feel someone else's pain; numerous experiments have shown that when we see someone else experiencing pain, it fires the same regions of our brains as are fired when we ourselves experience pain.[3] In fact, we have so much ability to experience another's pain that we're subject to emotional contagion, "catching" others' emotional states and internalizing them as our own. That's great when they're experiencing joy or enthusiasm—or when it propels us to rush to another's aid. But it can be a bad thing when others are feeling rage, pain, deep sadness, or hopelessness, which can create something researchers call *empathic distress*—or in layman's terms, burnout.

To insulate ourselves from feeling too much pain or negative emotion, we may withdraw from others. Studies have found that the longer students are in medical school, for example, the less empathy they demonstrate—with the greatest declines occurring as they begin working with real patients who are suffering and dying.[4]

One way that people tend to insulate themselves from empathic pain is to view the person in pain as a member of a different group than ourselves. The same brain scans that show we can feel someone else's pain also show that we tend to suppress our empathic responses when the person in pain is a member of an out-group (for example, a player on a different team) or someone we think deserved their pain (if, for example, we thought the other player was cheating during the game).[5]

Compassionate curiosity

Interpersonal curiosity works against both impulses. It also does something else that's vitally important and requires that we understand the difference between *empathy* and *compassion*, at least in psychological terms. *Empathy* is feeling *with* another person, while *compassion* is feeling *for* them—that is, being concerned for their well-being and wanting to help them, yet not necessarily mirroring or internalizing their emotions. Researchers sometimes express this distinction as *cognitive* versus *affective* empathy. When we experience *cognitive* empathy, we appreciate another's needs while maintaining sufficient emotional distance to serve as an objective partner in helping them solve their problems; when we experience *affective* empathy, we're more apt to get sucked into feeling another's emotions and pain, which ultimately can lead to distress, clouded judgment, and the need to withdraw from them. Brain scans, in fact, show that we activate different parts of our brains when we feel empathy versus compassion.[6]

Studies have found that we're more likely to help someone when feeling *compassion* for them versus experiencing empathic distress.[7] Perhaps even more important, compassion isn't simply a personality trait. Indeed, it's possible to *train* people to become more compassionate by engaging in what's called "loving kindness training," which often includes silent, meditative exercises in which participants visualize a person they feel close to and generate feelings of kindness toward them. Over time, they learn to generate the same feelings of kindness toward others, including strangers and even people with whom they have difficulties. After engaging in such training, participants are not only happier, they're also more likely to engage in altruistic behaviors.[8]

So, how can we use curiosity to foster better relationships? Here are some musings, ideas to ponder.

Musing #1: Put down our phones and just talk.

Let's start by not fooling ourselves into thinking that we're meaningfully connecting with others through social media. Sure, it can be a fun way to share photos and track down long lost cousins, but for the conversations that really matter, our tweets, texts, and posts aren't the stuff of true connection. If anything, they may just get in the way because we can find it easier to post something inflammatory on social media that we'd never say at a dinner party.

At your next dinner date with friends, you could play a little game: Put your phones on the table, and the first person to pick up their phone also has to pick up the tab. At work, you can ban phones and laptops from your meetings and encourage people to just talk, like we all did back in the old days—you know, way back in 2006.

At home, you can create "off hours" for your phones or try a "digital detox" on your next family vacation. A few years ago, my wife, our three daughters (two were teenagers at the time), and I did this on a road trip to New Mexico. Everyone either left their phones at home or packed them away in our bags to be looked at only once a day for a specified half-hour block of time. I only carried mine to find directions, before returning it to the glove box in the car.

Admittedly, early on, we experienced some symptoms of withdrawal—including, for me, feeling a phone buzzing in my pocket, then realizing my pocket was empty. After a few days, though, we all felt more at ease. My out-of-office reply for work emails worked just fine—my brief check-ins during our daily 30-minute digital reprieves proved that no one contacting me seemed to have needs that couldn't wait a week. At night, sitting beneath stunning Southwestern sunsets, our conversations were deep and rich—often touching on many of the topics raised in the Arons' 36 questions (though I didn't even know about them at the time). My daughters shared their aspirations for school, life, love, and happiness. And they asked my wife and me questions—about how we met, how we fell in love, and what we once thought we wanted to be when we grew up. With no phones in the landscape to interrupt us, we fell into a nightly tradition of selecting one member of the family and going around the table to share what we most admired about them. Often, we'd look around the restaurant and feel sad for the many people sitting around us, noses buried in their phones, who were dining alone together.

Musing #2: Ask one question a day that goes beyond the superficial.

Now that our phones are out of the way, let's *really* talk, going beyond the superficial and finding out what makes people tick—their experiences, values, and aspirations. Here's one simple way to take a conversation to a deeper level: Add two little words—*for you*—to any question. It works like this: What was the best moment of your family vacation . . . *for you?* What's the best part of your job . . . *for you?* What will be the most difficult aspect of this task . . . *for you?*

Tacking these two simple words onto a question—and giving adequate wait time—does two things. First, it helps people consider their own emotions, needs, and challenges. I've found sometimes it can create a sort of confessional experience; people will admit that maybe they're being too impatient, too risk-averse, or too leery of conflict. The second thing those two little words do is to show others you care enough to find out what's in their hearts and on their minds—in short, that you're curious about them.

Sure, it may feel more comfortable to chat about the weather, sports, or each other's jobs, but if we want to feel real connections with others, we can start by wondering what they *value, aspire to,* or *feel*. And we can use those two little words—*for you*—to draw those things out of others.

Musing #3: Appreciate each other.

Years ago, when Stephen Covey identified the habits of highly effective people, he called out their ability to "seek first to understand, then be understood."[9] In many ways, that statement captures what it means to be curious about others, though true *interpersonal* curiosity would take that advice one step further, prompting us to seek first to appreciate others. *Understanding*, by definition, means recognizing the full implications of something; if not wielded correctly, understanding may cause us to become dispassionate or dismissive of what someone feels or values. After all, psychopaths and con artists understand how other people feel—and then use that knowledge to manipulate them.

Appreciating, on the other hand, means recognizing the value of someone else's perspectives or emotions—both understanding how they feel and having their best interests at heart. So, true interpersonal curiosity entails appreciating another person's experiences, perspectives, values, and aspirations—and feeling kindness towards them. We don't have to agree with them, mind you; we may disagree, yet we can still appreciate how their experiences and emotions could lead them to a different perspective than ours, even as we resist the urge to cast them into an out-group and judge them.

The good news is that curiosity is innate in all of us, so it's unlikely anyone ever fully loses their interpersonal curiosity. Deep down, we're all curious; we like learning about other people. Also, we human beings are social creatures. We crave connecting with others in meaningful ways. Connecting those two dots—our need for connection and our innate curiosity—need not be complicated or difficult. That's not to say it's easy, either.

So, let's really appreciate each other—recognizing one another's *full worth*. We can start by recognizing empathy-killers in our own thinking—including labeling someone as a member of an out-group or perpetrators of their own suffering. True, people often make bad decisions that lead to their unhappiness. We all make mistakes. Once we get past that, we're better able to appreciate that no one is a "flat character"—we all have backstories that influence who we become, what we value, and where we want to go with our lives. As the adage goes, everyone has at least one book inside them. Curiosity can help us to find—and appreciate—what those stories might be.

I'm often struck by how many friends and couples share that when they first met, they couldn't stand each other, initially finding the other person to be annoying, conceited, uptight, boorish, or whatever adjective might apply. Over time, though, they came to appreciate each other—realizing one another's good qualities and that despite their superficial differences, they had a lot in common. So, what happened? Quite likely, they progressed through some version of the Arons' 36 questions, moving past *preferences* (which might be different) and beginning to share their values, aspirations, emotions, and regrets, which allowed shared appreciation to blossom and mutual dependency to develop as they solved each other's problems. The point here is to let curiosity propel us through these stages of getting to know, understand, and appreciate other people.

Connecting with curiosity

As mentioned earlier, the tragic murder of Kitty Genovese more than 50 years ago—and the seeming callousness of those who witnessed her death—sparked much soul searching about the decline of compassion in our increasingly urban society and led to academic inquiry into the bystander effect. An important detail omitted from the original telling of the story was that one neighbor, Sophia Farrar, had risked her own life to rush to aid Kitty, cradling her in her arms as she died. The subsequent narrative that our modern society had turned all of us into callous human beings with no connection, concern, or regard for one another, was never quite true.

We might take some solace in that. Rumors of the demise of our ability to develop and sustain meaningful connections with one another may have been greatly exaggerated. Nonetheless, the story struck a chord—likely stoking a reasonable fear that if we're not curious about one another, we *could* lose something as we transition from small communities to larger urban (and now digital) societies.

Moreover, we probably shouldn't be too quick to romanticize those tight-knit communities of yore as idyllic places where everyone got along and freely shared their deepest, darkest secrets. Such communities could also be stifling, oppressive places where values were more imposed than shared—as a great deal of American literature ought to remind us, including Nathaniel Hawthorne's *Scarlet Letter*, Harriet Beecher Stowe's *Uncle Tom's Cabin*, and Arthur Miller's *The Crucible*.

What interpersonal curiosity might allow us to do, though, is not necessarily go back to those places of imposed values and conformity, but instead help us discover new shared values and connections. Moreover, interpersonal curiosity could help us shift our focus from solely what other people *do* that gives them value, to consider instead what others feel, believe, and share with us.

Many writers, including columnist Barbara Ehrenreich from *The New York Times*, have lamented that Americans seem to suffer from a "cult of conspicuous busyness."[10] We define ourselves by those things that make us busy—our jobs, our kids' activities, and our accomplishments. Yet what often gets lost in our frenetic busyness and superficial information sharing about how busy, busy, busy we are may be the deeper conversations we all need to feel less lonely and more connected—conversations that often begin with chatting about our preferences but ultimately provide the opportunity to share our values and aspirations. As we'll soon see, it's connections with others that often serve as the source of true well-being and happiness. And as obvious as this sounds, it's a lesson that many people learn too late—or never at all. 💡

Curious for Good

CHAPTER THIRTEEN

The Search for Happiness

In late April 1991, Chris McCandless ventured alone into the Alaskan wilderness near Denali National Park on a quest to disconnect from society, be one with nature, and find deeper meaning in his life. For two years, since graduating from Emory University, he'd been on a curiosity-fueled odyssey. After ditching his car in the Arizona desert, he turned his back on his family (his father, in particular, who Chris had been distraught to learn had a secret second family in California), wealth, and privilege, and went off the grid as he hitchhiked and hopped freight trains across the American West. He lived with vagrants in Arizona, slept in a homeless shelter in Los Angeles, worked on farms in South Dakota, and kayaked down the Colorado River and into the Gulf of California, where he spent 36 days living off a five-pound bag of rice and whatever he could pull from the sea.

From what his biographer, Jon Krakauer, could discern from McCandless' journal, the young man hoped for Alaska to be his "final and greatest adventure"—where, "no longer poisoned by . . . civilization" he would "kill the false being within and victoriously conclude the spiritual revolution." After more than two months living off the land—hunting, fishing, and eating berries and other plants—he came to an epiphany while reading Leo Tolstoy's novella

Family Happiness and underlined these words in the crumpled paperback book he'd carried into the wild:

> He was right in saying that the only certain happiness in life is to live for others. . . . I have lived through much and now think I have found what is needed for happiness. A quiet life in the country, with the possibility of being useful to people to whom it is easy to do good . . . then work which one hopes may be of some use; then rest, nature, books, music, love for one's neighbor—such is my idea of happiness.

After living for many weeks in complete isolation, Tolstoy's words jumped off the page for McCandless, giving him a profound insight: that the key to happiness is *living for others*. The next day, July 3, he patched his jeans, shaved for the first time in months, photographed himself for posterity, packed his gear, and prepared himself to hike 20 miles back to civilization, concluding a long spiritual journey and rejoining humanity.

Tragically, he would never again see another person. The wilderness in which he had sought refuge seemingly turned on him, barring his return (the exact causes are not known; perhaps illness or flooded rivers). He died alone, in an abandoned bus deep in the woods, miles from another soul.

On one hand, we might view Chris's tragic fate as a cautionary tale of the perils of unrestrained youthful curiosity. Yet McCandless's intellectual and physical explorations helped him compress what others take a lifetime to learn (and many may never learn)—that only after we stop chasing pleasure and begin to appreciate the beauty around us and connect deeply with others can we find meaning and purpose in our lives. As we'll see, it's often when we reframe our pursuit of happiness that we achieve a sort of quiet contentment and sense of well-being.

Red, white, and the blues

Although the immoderate nature of McCandless's wanderings may have been unusual, what sparked it—an apparent gnawing emptiness inside—may hardly be unusual. Many Americans, despite having what in global terms amounts to staggering wealth, seem to feel a similar emptiness that leaves them searching for happiness in all the wrong places.

At first blush, Americans in general have been quite successful and living well. The U.S. is by far the world's wealthiest nation: With just 4.4 percent of the world's population, its citizens hold 41.4 percent of the world's total private wealth.[1] For many, the U.S. remains a land of opportunity, a place where ostensibly everyone has the right and freedom to pursue happiness and achieve the American dream—a big house, nice car, and vacations that stir the envy of our Facebook friends.

So, with all that financial bounty, we ought to be awash in happiness, right? After all, the predominant political discourse in the U.S. continues to focus on jobs and economic growth—as if feeling financially better off than we were a few years ago is the key to our happiness. If all that were true, with Americans' per capita income doubling since the 1960s,[2] we ought to be turning collective cartwheels of joy—or at least be a great deal happier than citizens in countries with more stagnant economies. So, are we?

Well, not exactly. Despite this income growth, Americans' reported happiness, compared with citizens of other developed countries, has remained flat. In recent years, despite continued increases in GDP, Americans are considerably less happy than they once were. Since 2007, when U.S. happiness ranked third among 23 Organization for Economic Cooperation and Development (OECD) countries surveyed, it has fallen to 19th of the 34 OECD countries currently ranked.[3] And a 2017 Gallup Organization survey that asked 130,000 people in 130 countries whether they had experienced positive emotions the day before (e.g., "Did you smile or laugh a lot yesterday?" "Did you learn or do something interesting yesterday?") placed America in the middle of the pack, behind people in impoverished places like Guatemala.[4]

Sadly, the U.S. is experiencing rising rates of drug addiction and suicide, and declining social trust. In fact, even as Americans' per capita income has risen, they have reported significant declines in social supports, freedom, charitable donation, and increasing feelings of living in a corrupt society. As it turns out, declines in these areas outweigh any positive effect on life satisfaction that greater income might bring. To offset, for example, the happiness effects of the loss of "social supports," Americans' per capita income would have to rise from $53,000 to $82,000. To offset the combined effects of the decline in all four variables, per capita income would have to rise from $53,000 to $133,000. So it's perhaps not surprising that the Nordic countries, which report greater happiness than the U.S., have lower per capita income yet far higher levels of personal freedom, social support, and perception of living in a society free from corruption.

Well, that's just survey data, you might say. People can lie on surveys, so maybe they don't tell us anything. That may be true. Yet in a variety of other measures, Americans' happiness seems to be fracturing. Since 2000, the percentage of Americans (of all ages) who binge drink (more than 5 drinks per day for men and 4 for women) has increased to the point that an estimated 16 million Americans (6 percent of the general population) now suffer from alcohol use disorder (compulsive use of alcohol and inability to regulate alcohol intake). Not coincidentally, emergency room visits related to heavy drinking have surged by 50 percent since the turn of this century and now account for 88,000 deaths each year in the U.S.[5] On top of that, after declining for three decades, the number of deaths from cirrhosis of the liver (a common result of excessive drinking) rose again in 2006. And then there are opioids. According to the Centers for Disease Control, more than 2 million Americans are addicted to pain killers (leading to 46 opioid overdose deaths per day in 2016)[6]; and as therapists note, many of these addictions have less to do with people seeking to numb physical pain as *emotional* pain.

Can money buy us happiness?

Of course, overall increases in American's *average* per capita income mask the reality that since the 1980s, only a small percentage of wealthy people have experienced substantial gains in personal income; meanwhile wages and wealth for the rest of Americans have stagnated or declined. Most notably, the top 1 percent of American households have made nearly all the gains in income and wealth in recent decades, while the share of the bottom half has plummeted. As a result, the top 1 percent of households now control 23 percent of income—equivalent to the bottom 70 percent. Indeed, while the U.S. remains the world's wealthiest nation, it's also its most inequitable in terms of both income and wealth. According to a report from retirement and financial services firm Allianz, on a scale of 0 to 100, with 0 being perfect equality and 100 being one person controlling all the wealth, the U.S. has a score of 80.6—the fourth highest, putting us in the dubious company of Turkey, Mexico, and Chile.[7]

So, it's entirely possible that a widening gulf between and haves and have-nots may be behind reported declines in American happiness—after all, psychologists have long observed that people feel happy when they believe they are keeping up with, if not outpacing, the Joneses. In simple terms, we feel happier when we perceive ourselves as better off than our family, friends, and neighbors, and conversely, less happy if we see others in our immediate circles faring better than us—a phenomenon that's exacerbated nowadays by social media, television reality programs, and advertising that makes us feel everyone else is better off than we are—from celebrities to friends to former classmates ("How does *that guy* have a boat?"). As a result, we may feel those income gaps even more acutely, and fall into a sort of collective funk.

Research, however, suggests another explanation for why America seems to remain so far from being the world's most satisfied nation. From the outset, let's acknowledge that being poor is no fun. There's proof of that: A synthesis of 11 studies of people's subjective well-being found that overall, people in richer nations were generally happier than those in poorer nations and that for people in impoverished nations, wealth corresponded with life satisfaction.[8] In other words, in places stricken with poverty, as people grow wealthier and pull themselves out of destitution, they report greater life satisfaction; in these circumstances, money *does* buy happiness.

Yet among people in wealthier nations, income becomes less predictive of life satisfaction. Beyond a certain point, incremental increases in personal wealth do not correspond with continued increases in happiness; after a point, gains in wealth often correlate with *declines* in happiness. Basically, wealth and happiness are correlated in a curvilinear fashion—a sort of inverted U—with increases in wealth correlating with increases in happiness as people move out of poverty, a leveling off at middle income levels, and a downward bend at higher income levels.[9] A number of studies have shown that after a point (an annual income of about $75,000 per year)[10] rising income becomes less important and even counterproductive to happiness as it becomes correlated with higher divorce rates, greater stress, and less time to enjoy the good things in life—in short, less overall well-being. As the researchers who synthesized these studies put it bluntly, "Our advice is to avoid poverty, live in a rich country, and focus on goals other than material wealth."[11] So, perhaps those philosophers and songwriters are partially right after all: Once we reach a modest level of income, money does *not* buy happiness.

With all of this in mind, it doesn't seem so surprising that the world's wealthiest nation isn't also its happiest one. Perhaps we have collectively reached a point of diminishing returns with our rising national income.

So, if material wealth (at least after a certain point) isn't the key to happiness, what is? To answer that question, we first need to understand the nature of happiness itself and how it comes to us in different forms, which, interestingly, reflect what we've been learning about different types of curiosity.

Different types of happiness

As far back as Aristotle, philosophers have observed that happiness takes different forms. For starters, there's *hedonic* happiness— sometimes known as pleasures of the flesh (e.g., eating, drinking, thrill seeking, and other delights). The trouble with this form of happiness, as philosophers and researchers alike have noted, is that it tends to wane over time—it has diminishing returns. That has a lot to do with our brain chemicals. As noted earlier, pleasure is associated with quick hits of dopamine, which fades just as quickly once it enters our brains, like neurochemical flash floods. As a result, we tend to experience diminishing returns with hedonic happiness as the novelty and the "buzz" of new experiences wears off, which leaves us seeking ever greater thrills to receive the same dopamine hit.[12] Many people, sadly, never seem to evolve beyond seeking only this form of happiness and as a result, wind up on what researchers and therapists alike refer to as a "hedonic treadmill."[13]

According to research, a deeper, more sustainable happiness can be found in *engagement*—feeling like we're getting better at things that matter to us, be it a hobby, profession, or other pursuit. A large body of research has, in fact, found a strong link between achieving goals and well-being. Interestingly, the strong link between happiness and engagement in goal attainment is consistent across cultures, regardless of whether they are predominately individualistic or collectivistic.[14] Finally, and perhaps most important, well-being appears strongly related to what Aristotle called *eudaemonia*—cultivating one's own virtues for the greater good. In simple terms, we might think of it as finding *meaning* or an altruistic purpose to our lives by helping others.[15]

At this point, we might ask, if we know so much about happiness, why do so many of us remain so miserable?

On the one hand, we might speculate that consuming a constant stream of advertising and other media, as many of us do, creates insatiable cravings, many of which we can never satisfy—be it tropical resorts, luxury cars, lobster dinners, or flat abs. We're constantly exposed to what we *don't* have (and often know we'll never get), which leaves many of us spinning on hedonic hamster wheels, never feeling satisfied or attaining a deeper sense of well-being.

So, what could help us step off the hedonic treadmill and find *real* happiness?

If we look to people who appear to find real happiness—who report being uncommonly happy—we find that they haven't followed common wisdom about *how* to be happy. That is, they're happy not because they're richer, sexier, or luckier. Rather, they appear to have cultivated something that many others lack. So, what is it? Well, as you might have guessed by now, it is, once again, curiosity—though a slightly different form of curiosity than what we've explored in previous chapters—a deeper, more reflective, and perhaps wiser form.

When curiosity makes us happy . . . and miserable

Let's start with the basics. We know from research that curiosity can spark little moments of delight that make life more enjoyable. One study found, for example, that people enjoyed listening to music more when they had no foreknowledge of what song they were about to hear next—that is, when each new (yet familiar) song came with a dose of anticipation—versus when they were told beforehand what song was coming next on a playlist.[16] This may explain why many of us prefer to listen to music in "random play" mode.

On the other hand, at times curiosity can rob us of our happiness by compelling us, against our better judgment, to seek information that causes us emotional pain. If, for example, we're told that someone has posted something negative about us on social media, learning *exactly* what they posted only serves to stir negative emotions, yet that's often exactly what people do. Studies in laboratory settings have found that people, in fact, tend to follow their curiosity to upsetting outcomes. Researchers Christopher Hsee and Bowen Ruan, for example, found that they could coax people into listening to the sound of nails on a chalkboard or looking at pictures of dog poop (boys will be boys, it seems) by creating a bit of mystery about which squares on a computer screen would yield a bland sound (water pouring into a glass) or innocuous image (of a stone) versus the distressing sound or revolting image. People could've clicked on none of the squares at all, yet when they were presented with "mystery squares," they were more likely to click on them.[17] In a subsequent study, Hsee and Ruan went a step further to see if people would touch electrified pens sitting on a table simply to see which ones would shock them.[18] They did, even though they had no reason at all to touch the pens besides simply being curious. From these experiments, Hsee and Ruan concluded that curiosity may not *always* be good for us.

Of course, these were rather superficial experiments. Seeing a picture of dog poop isn't going to leave us emotionally scarred for life; nor will listening to music on random play make our lives worth living. What we really want to know is whether, in *real life*, curiosity makes us happy—or miserable. Does curiosity make every day feel like an adventure, helping us uncover new opportunities, meet new friends, and discover new interests? Or could forms of morbid curiosity make us miserable, revealing the ugly truth about the world around us, rendering nothing sacred, and sending us into a downward spiral of stinking thinking, existential angst, and Ingmar Bergman film festivals?

From a scientific perspective, these are difficult questions to answer with precision—after all, there's no curiosity pill to offer one group while slipping another a placebo. Yet, as we'll see in the next chapter, if we knit together findings from several studies into a larger tapestry, something of a road map begins to emerge for how we can channel curiosity into a life well lived—a life that's less about thrills, excitement, and giddiness, and instead grounded in a deeper sense of satisfaction, well-being, and contentment. 💡

CHAPTER FOURTEEN

Curiously Happy

A few years after discovering the power of curiosity in creating better relationships, Todd Kashdan teamed up with Michael Steger, who himself had been studying how people find meaning in their lives. Steger had observed that happy people are often happy in ways that contrast with common images of happiness. Instead of filling their lives with lots of good things—"good feelings, good relationships, good desires, good vacations, good purchasing decisions, good plans for the future, good sex, good health, good looks"—Steger had observed that happy people accept that bad things happen and learn from them, using them as a springboard to achieving deeper insights and meaning in their lives.[1] So, in a sort of chocolate-mixing-with-peanut-butter experiment, the two researchers teamed up to explore whether *curious* people are happier in life—that is, do they experience greater life satisfaction and well-being?

Give me a C: What happens when college students are curious

Because both researchers were professors, they turned to a readily available population to study: college students, rounding up and surveying 97 of them on a variety of measures, including their *trait curiosity* (e.g., "I would describe myself as someone who actively seeks as much information as I can in a new situation"), *meaning and sense of life purpose* (e.g., "I have a good sense of what makes my life meaningful"), positive and negative *outlook on life*, their *personality traits* (extraversion, neuroticism, openness to experience, agreeableness, and conscientiousness), and *overall life satisfaction* (e.g., "In most ways my life is close to the ideal").[2] For 21 days, they tracked students' daily happiness and curiosity by asking them to track how *curious* they felt (e.g., "Everywhere I went, I was out looking for new things and experiences" and "When I was participating in activities, I got so involved that I lost track of time"), how much they engaged in *growth-oriented behaviors* (e.g., I "persevered at a valued goal even in the face of obstacles" or "expressed my gratitude for something someone did for me either verbally or in writing"), the extent to which they engaged in *hedonistic behaviors* (e.g., I "kept eating more than I intended of something just because it tasted so good" and I "had sex purely to get pleasure") and finally, their sense of *life meaning* (e.g., "How meaningful does your life feel?" and "How much were you looking to find your life's purpose?")

An interesting pattern emerged in students' daily tally of their curiosity and happiness. On days when they felt more *curious*, they also reported more persistence, goal directedness, and greater life satisfaction and meaning. The daily logs also revealed that students with more trait curiosity found less pleasure in hedonistic events than students with less trait curiosity. Although they still engaged in hedonistic behaviors (they were in college, after all), such activities were less apt to be the source of their happiness.

Not-so-curious students, by contrast, were *only* happy on days when they experienced hedonic pleasure. Overall, they also experienced *less* life satisfaction and life meaning. Curious students, on the other hand, experienced satisfaction even on days when hedonic "pleasure" passed them by; in short, they appeared to find joy in everyday intellectual exploration and the search for meaning. These findings led Kashdan and Steger to conclude that "curiosity is an important, neglected process in the pursuit of a life well lived."[3]

"Recharging" with curiosity

Years later, researchers in Spain conducted a similar, week-long study of 209 college students and discovered that curiosity put an extra spring in students' steps, basically recharging their batteries. Every afternoon over a five-day period, students responded to measures in these areas:

◊ *Life meaning* ("Today my life has a clear sense of purpose" and "Today I was searching for something that made my life feel significant").

◊ *State curiosity* ("Today I found myself looking for new opportunities to grow as a person" or became "so involved" in an activity "that I lost track of time").

◊ *Emotional state* ("At this moment, I feel happy" or "At this moment, I feel nervous").

Later, in the evening, students reported how *engaged* they felt with their studies (e.g., "At my studies, I feel strong and vigorous") and their *energy* levels (e.g., "At this moment, I feel emotionally drained from my studies"). Comparing these two data points revealed that the more curious students felt in the afternoon, the less exhausted they felt in the evening.[4] Curiosity seemed to energize them and help them sustain the sort of self-improvement and search for meaning that other studies suggest lie at the heart of life satisfaction.

Of course, one might argue that college students represent a narrow slice of the general population—not to mention a Frisbee-tossing, road-tripping, toga-wearing departure from the rest of our lives. So, what about ordinary people who live beyond the leafy confines of college campuses—real folks scraping together money to pay the mortgage, giving midnight teaspoons of cough medicine to sick kids, or running to catch the 6:52 a.m. bus to work? Does curiosity float their boats, too?

To answer this question, we'll zoom out a bit, taking a broader look at what people report on large-scale surveys of personality and happiness. One such study comes from a team of researchers that includes Martin Seligman, known for his groundbreaking work on "learned optimism" that linked how we explain our own successes and failures to our life success and happiness. For this examination, researchers mapped the results from more than 12,000 U.S. adults taking a scientifically validated survey of 24 personality traits (the VIA survey), onto results from a second survey of life satisfaction and happiness in all three forms: *hedonism*, *engagement*, and *meaning*.[5]

24 VIA Character Strengths	
Appreciation of beauty and excellence	Judgment
	Kindness
Bravery	Leadership
Creativity	Love
Curiosity	Love of learning
Fairness	Perseverance
Forgiveness	Perspective
Gratitude	Prudence
Honesty	Self-regulation
Hope	Social intelligence
Humility	Spirituality
Humor	Teamwork
	Zest
(www.viacharacter.org)	

By comparing the results of these two surveys, the researchers could identify which personality traits were most strongly linked to people's life satisfaction. Here they are, listed in rank order:

◊ Zest (approaching experiences with excitement and energy).

◊ Hope (expecting the best in the future and working to achieve it).

◊ Love (valuing close relations with others).

◊ Gratitude (being aware and thankful of the good things that happen).

◊ Curiosity (taking an interest in ongoing experience for its own sake).

Interestingly, curiosity ranked near the top of the list for all three types of happiness (seventh for *pleasure*, second for *engagement*, and fifth for *meaning*) which, upon further consideration, isn't all that surprising. When we're curious, we're likely to seek new experiences, which can support *hedonic* pleasure—for example, we might find a new favorite restaurant, band, or weekend pastime. Also, as we've seen, when we're curious we're more apt to cultivate and pursue personal interests, which supports *engagement*. Finally, when we're curious, we're more apt to discover deeper life purpose and *meaning*. The researchers also noted that people typically have not just one, but *multiple* personality strengths, which means that a personality trait like curiosity is likely to intertwine with, and amplify, positive aspects of other traits; for example, when combined, "zest and curiosity preclude boredom and anxiety."[6] In sum, curiosity appears to be positively correlated with life happiness for people of all age groups, well beyond their hacky-sack-playing days.

Does curiosity chase away the blues?

A similar but smaller study in Poland not only further bolsters the finding that curiosity supports life satisfaction, but also points to the intriguing possibility that in ways not fully understood, curiosity may serve to keep the blues at bay.[7] Researchers surveyed 257 people from ages 18–64 on measures of two types of curiosity: *stretching* ("Everywhere I go, I am out looking for new things or experiences") and *embracing* ("I am the type of person who really enjoys the uncertainty of everyday life") and compared their responses to answers on a separate survey that measured three dimensions of happiness: *enjoyment* ("My life is filled with pleasure"), *engagement*

("Most of the time I am fascinated by what I am doing"), *meaning* ("I have a very clear idea about my purpose in life"), and symptoms of *depression* (e.g., "During the previous week I had crying spells").

Among this sample, those who reported high levels of curiosity also reported high levels of pleasure, engagement, and meaning in their lives. Moreover, people with high levels of curiosity were also *less likely* to say they had felt depressed during the previous week. Correlation, of course, doesn't prove causation, so we shouldn't jump to the conclusion that curiosity wards off depression; it might work the other way around. Depression could, for example, *inhibit* curiosity; when we feel down we may be less likely to pick up a book or explore our environments. The research team speculated that a more complex, perhaps symbiotic relationship might be at play: When we're curious (and cultivate our curiosity), we may be more apt to seek new experiences, actively engage in new pursuits, and find deeper meaning in our lives. Having these factors present in our lives may help us to "counteract the tendency to focus attention on negative aspects of life," which, when unchecked, can lead to, or amplify, depression.[8] In other words, curiosity probably isn't a cure for acute depression, but might offer a form or preventive medicine, making us less likely to sink into depression or despair.

Curiosity and the U-shaped happiness curve

Curiosity may also help us navigate through emotional crises when we find ourselves at crossroads in our lives. For decades, studies of thousands of people from across the world—from different countries, cultures, and socioeconomic strata—have found a striking U-shaped curve in people's reported levels of happiness and well-being. Consistently, as people reach their 40s, their happiness begins to decline and keeps declining for a decade or so, until it begins to rise again in the their mid-50s.[9] In short, the midlife crisis is a documented phenomenon.

A common (though not necessarily universal) explanation for this dip in happiness, according to Aaron Jarden at Auckland University of Technology (who found a U-shaped curve in his surveys of more than 10,000 adults in New Zealand) is that "it's the time of life when people are more stressed, they have more responsibilities, both at work and for children. A lot of what impacts on the hedonic, or pleasurable, aspects of life takes a hit around that time."[10] Nevertheless, for most people in midlife, even as their hedonic happiness is falling, their eudemonic happiness begins to rise. For example, if you have children, Jarden notes, "You take a really big hit in your pleasure but a really big gain in sense of meaning and purpose." As a result, "your recipe for well-being around that time changes as well."[11]

In other words, life crises often force us to shift from one form of happiness to another. In midlife, for example, we may find that maintaining the physique we had as twentysomethings grows more difficult as our metabolism becomes less forgiving; thus, we find ourselves swearing off the foods and drink that once gave us pleasure (or consuming them with a side order of self-loathing). On top of that, we may discover that the things we had been striving for—the house on the cul-de-sac, the luxury car, the corner office— aren't as gratifying (or attainable) as we imagined, leaving us feeling unfulfilled and facing an existential crisis like that captured in the Talking Heads song "Once in a Lifetime":

And you may ask yourself
Where is that large automobile?
And you may tell yourself
This is not my beautiful house!

A friend once told me he'd had a "Talking Heads moment" when he realized the cement was drying on an imperfect relationship and unfulfilling future—for both him and his fiancée. So, in a moment of brave clarity, he broke off the engagement, trading certainty for uncertainty as he stepped into the unknown. As we'll see, how we respond to and navigate our way through crises like these "Talking Heads moments" has a lot to do with our ability to channel our curiosity to arrive at newfound clarity, direction, and purpose for our lives. For example, after my friend spent time reflecting and charting a different course for his life, he found his soul mate, landed a different job, and is now happily married with a beautiful family and a successful career.

Shifting our search for happiness

Studies suggest that many people—maybe even most of us—experience an emotional crisis at some point in our lives. A recent study of nearly 1,000 adults in the U.K., for example, found that 22, 24, and 14 percent of people aged 20–39, 40–59, and over 60, respectively, reported being in a time of crisis—an emotionally volatile span that lasted a year or more and overwhelmed their capacity to cope. During these crisis periods, they were left reexamining their lives and asking themselves soul-searching questions like, "Who am I, really?"[12]

It's precisely in these moments of crisis that the researchers found (and therapists note) that many people turn to a sort *self-curiosity* to reexamine their lives and recalibrate their personal formulas for happiness. In the U.K. study, for example, people in emotional crisis were more apt to report that they experienced higher levels of *intrapersonal* curiosity (reflecting on themselves and their past decisions), *perceptual* curiosity (seeking out new visual, auditory, and tactile experiences), and *epistemic* curiosity (reading self-help books, biographies, spirituality books, or books about health and diet).

In many ways, these curiosity-fueled emotional, intellectual, and spiritual quests help us to recalibrate our pursuit of happiness. Young adults, for example, may redirect their energies from pub crawls to figuring out what to do with the rest of their lives—looking for deeper *engagement* in work and other interests. Middle-aged people may realize that immersing themselves in work and striving for success has left them unfulfilled, so they may seek to rebalance their lives. And older adults, having checked other happiness boxes in their lives, may seek to find wisdom in quietude and contentment or in connections with others, such as their grandchildren. Perhaps one reason the stereotypical response to a midlife crisis—trading in a minivan for a sports car or a spouse of 20 years for someone 20 years younger—often seems pathetic is because instead of engaging in *reflective curiosity* that could lead to seeking deeper purpose and meaning in life, it represents what appears to be an incurious and shortsighted (and often self-destructive) effort to trade one hedonic pleasure for another.

In the next chapter, we'll see how, when channeled correctly, *reflective curiosity*—exploring our own emotions, motivations, and aspirations—can lead to powerful realizations, insights, and meaning. At the same time, we'll also see how *too much* navel gazing can keep us from discovering what's often the shortest route to our happiness: getting outside of our own heads, taking a good look around, and seeing that what we need to be happy has often been right there in front of us all along. ☙

CHAPTER FIFTEEN

A Wonderful Life

Most of us spend most of our waking hours tracking over pretty much the same ground—driving the same route to work, walking the same office hallways, or taking our dog on the same loop through the neighborhood. So, when we inadvertently take a wrong turn on the way to work, get off on the wrong floor, or reverse our usual loop with the dog, it may be disorienting when we suddenly find ourselves somewhere we've never been before—even if it's just one street off our normal route, one floor away from where we normally spend our waking hours, or one block away from home. At other times, a familiar place can suddenly look unfamiliar when we see it from a different side of the street. It's almost as if we're seeing it again for the first time.

All these experiences can leave us wondering, *How have I never seen this place before?* We may also delight in discovering something we've never seen before—like a new sidewalk café, a new piece of office décor, or a tree in bloom. As it turns out, the joy we find in making these small discoveries—closing knowledge gaps we didn't even know we had—may actually be therapeutic.

Take a look around . . . and inside

Years ago, a group of English therapists and researchers attempted to apply this concept in an unusual experiment with war veterans who were experiencing post-traumatic stress, children in poverty, and older adults suffering from memory loss. In this small-scale yet in-depth study, they sought to help these patients use curiosity to turn familiar places into unfamiliar ones, uncovering erstwhile unseen beauty in the world around them—and more contentment in themselves. Altogether, 27 people participated in the project, which was part of a larger, community-wide program called the Liverpool Decade of Health and Wellbeing, which encouraged people to, among other things, take notice of familiar places, seeing them through new eyes.[1] The idea was to enable participants to create their own "therapeutic spaces" or settings that encourage rejuvenation. Typically, such places include forests, beaches, retreats, spas, and sacred places. For the Liverpool project, however, the goal was to help people turn their own urban environments into therapeutic spaces by seeing them in a new light—with *curiosity*—and in so doing, turn seemingly ordinary places into extraordinary ones. In short, they hoped to help people experience the same sense of well-being they might feel when admiring a mountain, studying a painting, or watching waves crash onto a shoreline.

One such effort manifested as the Veterans' Photography project, which taught war survivors to think like photographers, capturing authentic glimpses of life, even in the mundane. For many of the ex-servicemen who entered the program encased in a shell of machismo, photography offered a safe way to express their emotions. One veteran, for example, photographed a picture of a tree growing out of a wall, which he found particularly poignant given his cancer diagnosis. Afterward, in discussion groups, as people talked about the photographs they'd taken, they offered a sort of "sideways mirror" for viewing their lives, giving them a way to step outside themselves and reflect on their own emotions and circumstances in a different light.

As photography made them more curious about the world around them, they also became more curious about their inner worlds. Often, as one veteran put it, photography helped them search for the truth "no matter how shit the truth was." Thus, curiosity improved their well-being because it encouraged them to, in the words of the same veteran, stop "bottling up" things inside themselves because they were "too stubborn . . . to see another person's point of view." In many ways curiosity—in this case, *reflective curiosity* about others' and their own feelings—offered a path out of the briar patch of their own tangled emotions and toward something resembling happiness.

Looking in all the wrong places

Looking inward to sort out our own feelings and emotional entanglements makes sense, of course. After all, we cannot expect others to make us happy if we're not first happy with ourselves. Moreover, if we keep negative emotions trapped inside, they tend to eat away at us, metastasizing like a cancer and eroding our happiness. Yet when it comes to creating happiness, we might encounter limits—or at least experience diminishing returns—to our inner journeys of reflective curiosity. In her book, *America the Anxious: How Our Pursuit of Happiness Is Creating a Nation of Nervous Wrecks*, Ruth Whippman observes that Americans' obsession with happiness appears to be making us miserable. As a Brit transported to sunny California—where seemingly everyone expects to be happy (and fret that something's wrong with them if they're not)—she finds Americans talking about their efforts to achieve happiness everywhere she goes—on the playground, in the supermarket, and the doctor's office. She also notes that Americans spend lavishly on self-help books and seminars, spawning a billion-dollar industry to teach ourselves how to be happy.[2] Yet it doesn't seem to be working.

One reason happiness may remain so elusive, she speculates, could simply be that the more we dwell on feeling happy, the less happy we feel. To wit: A study at the University of California, Berkeley, invited two groups of people to report how happy they felt after watching a feel-good film. One group had previously read a short article on the importance of happiness; the other group read the same article with the words "accurate judgment" substituted for happiness. As it turned out, the group who *didn't* read the article on happiness were *more likely* to report feeling positive emotions after watching the film, leading the researchers to conclude that "wanting to be happy may make people lonely."[3] Or in Whippman's words, "Like an attractive man, it seems the more actively happiness is pursued, the more it refuses to call and starts avoiding you at parties."[4]

Looking to others

Another reason happiness may avoid us could be, as Whippman asserts, because we keep looking for it in the wrong places—namely, *inside* ourselves. Whether it's the perky social media memes (e.g., "Happiness should not depend on other people" and "Happiness is an inside job"), weekend journeys of self-discovery, or the uniquely American practice of cherishing "me time," we seem to have embraced a decidedly "isolationist" path to happiness.[5] As if we needed to spend more time alone. Already, Americans eat half of their meals by themselves and our teenagers spend less time hanging out with friends than any other generation in history (trading face time for screen time).[6]

But the real shortcoming of an "isolationist" approach to happiness may be that it runs counter that what decades of research have shown: *Happiness depends on other people*—or more precisely, on *helping* other people. According to an exhaustive review of research by Richard Ryan and Edward Deci (two giants in the field of positive psychology), the factor most consistently linked to personal happiness is alternatively called *attachment* or *relatedness*; decades of research show that relationship-enhancing personality traits consistently rank near the top of attributes correlated with subjective well-being.[7]

Not surprisingly, a Gallup worldwide survey of people's happiness discovered that individual well-being is strongly linked to the *presence of social networks*—which may explain why people in less well-to-do Latin American countries, like Guatemala, report, on average, greater day-to-day happiness than Americans.[8] Introverts take heart: The *quantity* of social interactions isn't as important as the *quality* of those interactions; a study of 280 college students, for example, found happiness to be strongly correlated with friendship, even if students reported having just one best friend.[9]

Turning curiosity into happiness

Let's take stock of what we've learned to now ponder how we can translate curiosity into a greater sense of well-being and life satisfaction.

Musing #1: Find your wonder.

A couple years ago, while giving a talk about the power of curiosity to a group of statewide education leaders in Michigan, I had a brief but meaningful conversation during a break with then-state superintendent of schools, the late Brian Whiston. I shared with Whiston that my eldest daughter was enrolling in college but was still undecided about her major. "Ask her what problem she wants to solve," he replied. I thought that was an interesting and compelling way to frame a college education—around curiosity. So, I carried his advice back to her. As it turns out, his advice also reflects a key finding from Gallup's worldwide survey of happiness—across the globe, on days when people feel most happy, it's often because they "learned something" the day before. Recall also that college students were happier and more energized on days when they were curious. In short, we appear to be happiest when we're learning—when we're pursuing knowledge that lies just over the horizon.

It's great to frame academic or professional pursuits around big, essential questions, but that's not always possible to do. So, take heart: We can still feel energized and fulfilled by pursuing more simple or practical questions, like, How can I grow better tomatoes this summer? How might I redecorate my home on the cheap? How can I talk to my teenager? (Or, if you're a teenager, How can I talk to my parents?) Basically, we're happier when we have mysteries—be they large or small—to pursue.

Musing #2: Stop, look, and listen.

Perhaps the most powerful insight to emerge from the Veterans' Photography project in Liverpool is that simply looking at things in a different light can make our surroundings new again and provide us with small moments of joyful discovery. By using a photographer's eye to look more closely at places familiar to us, we're apt to see something new—a flowering tree, an artfully manicured shrubbery, a neighbor whose quiet kindness we view with admiration.

We can also listen closely—hearing sounds we've never noticed before, which in turn could leave us wondering, What is that? A frog? A locust? Where are they? If we allow ourselves to experience a childlike sense of wonder about the world around us, we become everyday explorers constantly experiencing the joy of discovery, which is, of course, the essence of curiosity.

My grandmother was one of the happiest, most content people I've known. She lived on the same farm in Iowa her entire adult life. She probably spent 90 percent of her time in a one-square-mile area around the farmhouse, leaving only once a week or so for a pilgrimage to town to get groceries, get her hair done, and run other errands. In the twilight of her life, her daughters hoped she might move to town where she'd be safer, but she stayed put. Now I understand why. When I was in college, I exchanged monthly handwritten letters with my grandmother. Though her life seemed rather placid and simple to me, as a young man who'd ventured far from home to see the world, she could fill pages with descriptions of the changing seasons, migrating wildlife, and small happenings around the farm. For her, her small corner of world was *always* changing and piquing her curiosity because she could appreciate the smallest of tiny details and thus see her surroundings anew every day—the flowers blooming, the birds at her window, the thunderheads forming across the cornfields.

Musing #3: Be open to experience.

The first two musings above reflect the power of being *actively* curious—asking questions and looking at the world around us through a lens of curiosity. Yet there's another powerful aspect of curiosity that's equally important to our happiness—something called *openness to experience* or embracing novel experiences, engaging in personal growth, and responding to life's unexpected twists and turns with grace and humor.[10] This form of curiosity can make even painful experiences more bearable when we we're able to say to ourselves, "OK, so that happened . . . what should I learn from that?"

Viewing the vicissitudes of life with curiosity can also tamp down our anxieties about what may happen in the future, because we figure, no matter the outcome, we'll pick ourselves up, dust ourselves off, and emerge a bit wiser. Reflecting upon his many studies of curiosity and happiness, Todd Kashdan concluded, in fact, that this ability to roll with the punches may be the most important key to happiness. We encounter disappointments and uncertainties in our lives, so "We need to believe that we can handle that novelty and that uncertainty, and if we don't feel that we can handle it, we're not going to feel curious; we're going to feel confused or we're going to feel threatened."[11]

Musing #4: Be curious for others.

Perhaps the most important lesson to draw from this research is that we're happiest when we're helping other people. As we've seen, on one level, curiosity can draw us closer to others, helping us learn what makes them tick and feeling compassion (or loving kindness) for them. Yet on a more sublime level, we consider Aristotle's concept of *eudaemonia*—cultivating our virtues for the greater good—to contemplate what it would be like to cultivate our own *curiosity* for the greater good. On this level, curiosity is apt to deliver the greatest sense of fulfillment and meaning. We are not chasing horizons or pursuing questions for our *own* joy of discovery, but rather, to find answers that help others—for example, becoming a better parent (or teacher or coach), helping others work through their problems, or solving a vexing challenge for our coworkers, clients, customers, or patients.

Happiness is right under our noses

Chris McCandless appears to have discovered the true nature of happiness deep in the Alaska wilderness only after swearing off the typical hedonic pleasures of most young men his age—trading bars and pizza parlors for berries and small game—and immersing himself in the challenge of surviving in the wild. Could he have uncovered the same insight by reading Tolstoy or the many studies cited here? Perhaps. Yet few of us learn life's lessons that way. Instead, we often must experience them and learn them ourselves. Only then do words jump off the pages of a book and speak to us—or does the advice of a loved one or friend resonate with us. In the end, perhaps only after exhausting the other forms of happiness could McCandless fully appreciate that the key to happiness lies in connecting with and helping other people. Sadly, his epiphany came too late, after he'd already removed the guardrails from his life.

In many ways, McCandless's short life reflects curiosity burning brightly—an insatiable wanderlust entwined with dewy aspirations to emulate his hero, Henry David Thoreau, in living life to its fullest. We might see his tragic end as a cautionary tale about curiosity, the modern equivalent of Pandora or Eve. Yet for his biographer, Jon Krakauer, himself an avid mountaineer who understood the impulse to lead a life less ordinary, Chris's tragic story and sophomoric writings stirred not contempt, but compassion, as he saw in McCandless a portrait of himself as a young man.

If the studies of people in the U.K. are any indication, at some point in our lives, most of us will likely experience a similar sort of emotional crisis when we wonder what it's all about—and attempt (perhaps in less dramatic fashion) to chase horizons and escape a frenetic and callous society through some form of quietude and reflection where we hope to find the meaning of it all. It's in these times that curiosity can be a consort—helping us to reflect on our lives, dive deeply into new experiences to escape a rut, find new joy in our surroundings, and perhaps, most importantly, reach out to, and connect with, people around us. 💡

Civic Curiosity

CHAPTER SIXTEEN

The Divided States of America

Matthew Horn, a software engineer from Boulder, Colorado, said he canceled plans to be with family in Texas for Christmas after the election of Donald Trump—not because he was too busy, couldn't afford the trip, or wanted a white Christmas, but because he feared the political conversations that might emerge over the chestnuts roasting on an open fire. He was hardly alone. After the 2016 election, people on both sides of the political divide said they felt alienated by family members who held different political views— those who leaned left said they were tired of being labeled "liberal elites" and those who leaned right took umbrage at being labeled "racists."[1]

Like a flag flapping too long in the wind, America seems to be tearing apart at the seams. According to a recent Gallup survey, Democrats and Republicans have never been further apart on key issues of government regulation, government waste, aid to the poor, and same-sex marriage; across all issues, the average percentage gap in views between people who identify with or lean Republican or Democratic is now 36—greater than any other divide (class, race, or gender) and a sharp increase of 21 points since these polls began 23 years ago.[2]

New studies show that animus toward people of a different political persuasion is greater than ever, with people of both parties harboring strong partisan stereotypes, assuming the best of members of their own party and the worst of members of the other party; studies have found, for example, that partisan stereotypes tend to be just as strong as racial ones, with more people taking an increasingly dim view of people in other parties.[3] On top of that, dating websites report that people are now more likely to choose a mate based on their political preference than their physical attributes or personalities. Meanwhile, voter registration data show that residential neighborhoods are becoming increasingly homogeneous along party lines.[4] In short, Americans appear to be retreating into political tribes, quick to judge and cast aspersions on people in other parties. Forget the Montagues and Capulets; if Shakespeare were penning *Romeo and Juliet* today, coming from families of different political persuasions could be sufficient to make them star-crossed lovers.

While the current partisan rancor may be distressing, we might find some solace in knowing that it isn't all that new in American culture. In many ways, the present divide represents a productive tension that exists in any democracy; something baked in—and evident—from the start of the new republic. In fact, almost two centuries ago, Alexis de Tocqueville, a young French aristocrat, toured the continent and observed the tribalism and mistrust emerging in the young nation's political parties, and worried the spreading tribalism could rip the country apart—or pave the way for a subtle yet pernicious "tyranny of the majority" that could quash democracy without a shot being fired.

However, he also saw hope for the young nation. He predicted, with remarkable clairvoyance, that America would become one of two great nations in the world—due in large part to an infectious disposition and attitude of curiosity that seemed deeply ingrained in the American psyche and spread quickly to newcomers.

Alexis de Tocqueville encountered curiosity everywhere he went in America: in the wanderlust, inventiveness, and unwavering optimism of its citizens, and in their belief that their best days still lay ahead, which drew them together to build schools, roads, and canals. He caught glimpses of curiosity when people invited him into their homes and log cabins to discuss the news of the world. He saw it in the staggering proliferation of free and independent newspapers in nearly every village and hamlet. And he heard it in the echoes of the nation's religious beginnings, which served to temper the citizens' industriousness with the better angels of compassion and altruism.

America, according to Tocqueville, was a nation filled with curious people, and this uniquely American character trait gave the young French tourist hope that America might someday fulfill its ideals of a free society that treated all citizens as equals.

Curiosity, as we've seen, can go dormant in individuals. So, too, it may go dormant in a people. Yet it's likely still there, waiting to be summoned. And tapping into a collective sense of curiosity—about ideas, principles, and each other—may hold the key to repairing what appears to be a growing rift in our society and perhaps the best way to avoid the dark future that the young Frenchman—now regarded as one of the history's most insightful political philosophers—worried could befall democratic societies, not just in America, but around the world.

Land of the easily duped?

Fast forward nearly two centuries. In the weeks before the 2016 presidential election, Facebook and other social media sites were abuzz with stories from across the political spectrum about Pope Francis endorsing Donald Trump, ISIS leaders calling for American Muslims to vote for Hillary Clinton, and Mike Pence labelling Michelle Obama a vulgar woman. We know now, of course, that these were all false stories propagated by unscrupulous organizations and individuals seeking to influence voters; nonetheless, this "fake news" received more engagement and reposts than news from traditional media outlets like CNN, *The New York Times*, and *The Washington Post*,[5] touching off a firestorm of criticism of Facebook and the algorithms it used to increase the popularity of these stories to sell more ads.[6]

After the election, it became apparent that Russia had attempted to compromise our democracy by flooding social media outlets with erroneous information manufactured by Russian "trolls" and Macedonian teenagers who created "click bait" stories to push into social media feeds.[7] However, amid all the furor over Russia, Facebook, trolls, and fake news and the collective gasp of "How could they?" few people bothered to ask a deeper and perhaps more important question: "How could *we*?" That is, how could so many people on both sides of the political divide have been so easily duped? After all, many of the stories were patently absurd or could have been easily fact-checked before forwarding or reposting them. Yet when MIT researchers studied the spread of 126,000 rumors on Twitter, they found false news stories spread much "farther, faster, and deeper" than the truth—not because of bots or trolls, but because of average, ordinary Americans spreading them.[8] So, what were all these people thinking?

One possibility is that they weren't thinking much at all. After all, many people use social media for entertainment, not earnest research, deep introspection, or philosophical debate. So, those Facebook, Twitter, and Instagram followers may have simply been blithely "liking" things that appeared in their news feeds without giving them much further consideration (or even reading them).

A second possibility, though, is that they were afflicted with what cognitive scientists call *confirmation bias*—the propensity to accept information that supports our view and disregard data that doesn't. As cognitive psychologist Daniel Kahneman explains, *disbelieving* something is harder than believing it because skepticism requires us to kick our brains into high gear—into effortful, slow-thinking mode. For example, in a clever experiment, psychologists found that when they taxed people's "slow-thinking" brains by asking them to hold a number sequence in memory and then presenting them with a nonsensical statement, like "A dinca is a flame," people were more apt to proclaim the absurd statement to be true than when they could simply focus on the statement. In other words, disbelieving erroneous information—be it a nonsensical statement or false news—requires that we take our brains out of their default, low-effort mode and keep them revved up in high-effort thinking.[9]

A third possibility for why people might be so easily beguiled by false news reflects the heart of social media itself—namely, that it's *social*. False news stories were never explicitly offered up from Yuri in Moscow or Dimitri in Macedonia; rather, they came to us via friends and family—members of our own social groups. By nature, most of us find it difficult, if not downright impossible, to contradict our social groups and say something that might offend or elicit opprobrium from them. So, we tend to go along with the group.

Political groupthink under the microscope

Studies have shown that people (on both sides of the political divide) tend to more-or-less blindly accept what they surmise other members of their social groups accept—and reject what their group rejects. A Yale University study,[10] for example, presented self-identified liberal and conservative college students with two versions of a social welfare policy—one that offered generous benefits and the other, scant benefits. When presented with the two policy briefs in an unvarnished manner—with no reference to partisan views or political ideology—not surprisingly, liberal students preferred more robust benefits while conservative students preferred less generous benefits.

However, when researchers gave the experiment a false news twist—telling liberal students that it was Democrats who *opposed* more-generous benefits (for being "only a band-aid effort") and Republicans who *supported* more-generous benefits (for "supporting a basic work ethic and sense of personal responsibility"), liberal students suddenly became more likely to *oppose* more lavish benefits to welfare recipients. Afterward, the students insisted that they arrived at their position based on the "details of the proposals" and their own "philosophy of government"—and that their own party's position had nothing to do with it. The researchers fooled conservative students just as easily. When they told conservative students that Democrats supported skimpier benefits for welfare recipients and Republicans wanted more robust ones ($200 vs. $800 per month) the right-leaning students decided overwhelmingly that *more generous* handouts for poor people made sense.

In a final version of this experiment, researchers presented two groups of liberal students with a policy proposal (a federally funded job-training program) that a previous focus group of liberal students had endorsed. One group read about the program with no political commentary, while the other learned (falsely) that Democrats *opposed* the program. Both groups of students were then asked to write editorials in which they could choose to argue in favor of or against the program. The liberal students who had read about the jobs programs with no commentary overwhelmingly supported it (76 percent wrote editorials in favor), yet when told Democrats opposed it, the overwhelming majority of self-professed liberal students (71 percent) wrote articles opposing it.

What may be most striking about this study is that in all cases, students had plenty of time and opportunity to think deeply about the policy proposals; in short, as the researchers put it, "their attitude change did not result from mindless conformity." In fact, through prompts and opportunities for reflection, the researchers sought to encourage students to kick their brains into a high-gear, effortful, slow-thinking state. Nonetheless, group affiliation appeared to hold more sway over their beliefs than their own thought processes. Indeed, many students appeared to engage in complex mental contortions to rationalize their position. Liberal students who were told that Democrats opposed the jobs program argued, for example, that it would "dump beneficiaries into menial labor."

In short, even well-educated students at one of the nation's most prestigious institutions find it difficult to buck groupthink and operate as independent, critical thinkers. Sadly, colleges and universities—the place where we expect students to sharpen their thinking abilities—often do little to help students develop their critical thinking abilities. A recent analysis of 2,300 undergraduates at 24 institutions, for example, found that fully 45 percent of students demonstrated no significant gains in critical thinking, complex reasoning, and writing during their first two years of college.[11] A study of 32,000 college students arrived at much the same figure: that fully 40 percent of students demonstrated only basic or below-basic levels of critical thinking skills.[12] Why should this be?

As it turns out, the problem may be deeply rooted in the wiring of our brains.

Opinions first, facts second

A general finding to emerge from cognitive science over the past few decades is that we all tend to form opinions first, then find facts and logic to support our opinions afterward. That may be because our more primitive limbic brains—home to emotions and unconscious responses to our environment—are far more powerful than our more sophisticated prefrontal cortexes—home to logic and conscious thought. Social psychologist and researcher Johnathan Haidt uses the metaphor of an *elephant* and *rider* to describe the interaction between these two parts of our brains. Our logical, conscious brain wants to think it's in charge, but it's often a mere rider atop the elephant of our emotions and unconscious responses to our environment; sometimes the rider controls the elephant, but for the most part, the elephant pretty much goes where it wants to go.[13]

As a result, for people standing on either side of the political divide, inserting more facts into a debate seldom brings them together. If anything, the facts may only serve to polarize them further. Several studies have shown that it's often people who are *most engaged* in effortful thinking—whose "riders" are the busiest—who also tend to be the most politically polarized about facts on a variety of issues including gun control and climate change.[14] For example, in a study involving 1,759 parents, researchers presented the parents with widely accepted science that debunks the myth that childhood vaccines cause autism. After absorbing these facts, most parents accepted that, the opinions of Hollywood celebrities and discredited scientists notwithstanding, vaccines do *not* cause autism. However—and here's where things get confusing—parents who entered the study wary of vaccines emerged from the study *less likely* to vaccinate their children *even though they accepted* the science that showed no link between vaccines and autism.

How could that be? Quite likely, as the researchers concluded, these parents simply conjured up "other concerns about vaccines to defend their pre-existing anti-vaccine attitudes."[15] It seems that deeply ingrained ideas—in this case, distrust of vaccines—can be like zombies; we can kill them with facts, but they find a way to come back to life again.

Facts don't bring us together

In a recent study involving thousands of subjects with the aim of figuring out how to make science films appeal to a broad audience (that is, people of both political persuasions), Yale professor Dan Kahan and colleagues unearthed a similar phenomenon: Facts often have little to do with people's opinions. From the outset of the study, they found, unsurprisingly, that self-identified Republicans and Democrats viewed two hot-button issues—climate change and fracking—quite differently. As we might expect, right-leaning subjects were *less likely* than their left-leaning counterparts to believe there's "solid evidence" of humans causing climate change or that fracking poses a risk to people's health.[16]

Perhaps more surprising was that those with *greater science knowledge* weren't any closer, but rather, further apart in their opinions on these issues. The better people scored on a test of science knowledge (responding to questions like "Antibiotics kill viruses as well as bacteria: true or false" and "Which gas makes up most of the Earth's atmosphere? Hydrogen, nitrogen, carbon dioxide, oxygen") the more their ideologies held sway—the more ardent and divergent they were in their views. At the other end of the scale, those with scant science knowledge held pretty much the same opinion on these issues—a sort of shrugging *meh* response to the question of whether global warming or fracking poses a risk to human health. Charting people's views with their levels of science knowledge revealed that as people become more scientifically literate, their views increasingly diverge—with liberals becoming increasingly alarmed about fracking and climate change and conservatives becoming increasingly dismissive of both, viewing them perhaps as hoaxes or minor issues blown out of proportion.

Basically, what the researchers confirmed was something called "politically motivated reasoning"—a well-documented phenomenon that shows people tend to form opinions first and then find facts to support them. Why should that be? Well, as the researchers noted, most people perceive fewer risks in making a bad choice in the voting booth (after all, it's but one vote among many and something done, at best, once every other year) than in being alienated or ostracized in a social group—something they must deal with in a personal way every day. As a result, it's easier for people to decide, to paraphrase the old Luther Ingram song, "If loving my partisan views is wrong, I don't wanna be right."

Please don't confuse me with your facts

What's worse is that most people don't even want to *learn* what the other side thinks. In studies of hundreds of people in Canada and the U.S., researchers found that fully two-thirds of them—from both sides of the political divide—turned down a chance to win extra money simply because they *didn't want to hear* opposing ideas or data about contentious issues like same-sex marriage, presidential elections, marijuana, climate change, gun control, and abortion.[17] In most cases, people admitted that they knew little about the other side's position. Still, they had no desire to hear it because they feared it might stir up feelings of anger or cause them to say something hurtful. So, they opted to stay in their own ideological bubbles, thank you very much. Reporting on their findings in the *Los Angeles*

Times, the researchers observed that "It's a scary situation if, in this deeply partisan moment in U.S. history, the one thing both sides have in common is a lack of curiosity about what the other thinks."[18]

Scary indeed.

Let's take a moment to review what we can glean from these studies:

◊ Our political views tend to be more tribal than logical.

◊ Facts do little to change our views.

◊ Most people don't want to hear what the other side thinks.

None of this bodes well for democracy. If we're afraid to listen to other views, unable to gather facts to rethink our own opinions, or venture beyond our ideological tribes to seek compromise, we might wonder if democracy can survive. Indeed, if democratic debate is replaced with warring factions attempting to talk over and drown one another out, we might fear sliding into what most troubled Tocqueville—that our democracy could morph into a "tyranny of the majority," ruling not with the iron fist of oppression and deprivation, but the "soft despotism" of groupthink, where dissenters, fearful of being cast out of mainstream society, simply stay quiet. Fortunately, as we'll see in the next chapter, all hope is not lost. ☙

CHAPTER SEVENTEEN

Curiosity and Democracy

When Alexis de Tocqueville set sail for America in 1831, his journey was born out of both wanderlust and necessity. Slight of stature but prodigious of mind, Tocqueville grew up during the tumultuous years of the Napoleonic era and return of the monarchy in 1815. Born into the aristocracy (his parents both narrowly escaped the guillotine), his education initially instilled in him devotion to the church and the monarchy. As a teenager, though, his "insatiable curiosity" drew him to the writings of French enlightenment authors like Montesquieu and Voltaire. Their "radical" ideas about freedom of speech, freedom of religion, and separation of church and state left him questioning his early lessons and feeling like he'd "been through an earthquake."

Privately, he believed the arc of history would bend toward free, democratic societies. Outwardly, though, he maintained the façade of a respectable aristocrat and secured, with his father's help and royal connections, an appointment as a magistrate in Versailles—a cushy position until the July Revolution of 1830 overthrew Charles X and put Louis-Phillipe, the so-called "Citizen King," in power as the head of a new constitutional monarchy. Though Tocqueville pledged fealty to the new government, he was treated with suspicion and demoted without pay. Cast adrift, he decided to set sail for the New World, ostensibly to study the prison system in America along with a friend, another displaced aristocrat, Gustave de Beaumont.

With Beaumont, Tocqueville traveled across North America, from the Atlantic coast of New England to the western hinterlands of Michigan, up to chilly Montreal and down to balmy New Orleans. Like many visitors to the United States, he was at once enthralled and appalled by what he saw. He admired Americans' ability to come together to build schools, create roads, serve on juries, and solve civic problems, and he marveled at how Americans faced the future, not the past. For example, when he asked a sailor in Rhode Island why American ships weren't built to last, the sailor replied in a manner befitting modern Silicon Valley entrepreneurs: Rapidly changing naval technology meant ships built today would soon be obsolete, so why build them to last?

He also alternately admired and was taken aback by Americans' restless curiosity. "In the United States," he wrote in the first volume of his now famous tome, *Democracy in America*, "a man builds a house to spend his latter years in it and he sells it before the roof is on." An American, he observed, was constantly on the move. The vast openness of the continent seemed to beckon to everyone: "If at the end of a year of unremitting labor [an American] finds he has a few days' vacation, his eager curiosity whirls him over the vast extent of the United States, and he will travel fifteen hundred miles in a few days." In many ways, Americans seemed to live a life of boundless curiosity, in a perpetual "chase of that complete felicity which is forever on the wing."

Everywhere Tocqueville went in America, he also heard something largely absent in France: an entrepreneurial spirit. Unlike Frenchmen of the 19th century who were hemmed in by social class and expected little change in their fortunes, Americans all seemed to be eagerly looking to get ahead and constantly looking for ways to turn a buck. "As one digs deeper into the national character of the Americans," he wrote to a friend, "one sees that they have sought the value of everything in this world only in the answer to this single question: how much money will it bring in?" As he observed in *Democracy in*

America, "I know of no country, indeed, where the love of money has taken stronger hold on the affections of men."

Because of all this, Tocqueville predicted, quite sagely, that the fledging nation would one day be "one of the greatest peoples of the world" alongside one other nation: Russia. All other nations in the world, he surmised, had reached their zenith. Only Russia and America were proceeding "along a path to which no limit can be perceived."

Yet not always so free . . . or curious

Yet Tocqueville was also appalled and disturbed by numerous contradictions in Americans, starting with their imperfect conception of equality, including how men treated their daughters and wives. By his reckoning, women in America traded the prison of their father's home for the cloister of their husband's. He was also appalled by the white majority's treatment of people of other ethnicities. When he arrived in Memphis, for example, he observed a scene that "one couldn't watch without feeling one's heart wrung." A band of Choctaw Indians, recently displaced from their homeland, were loaded onto a flatboat that would carry them to the Oklahoma territory, their dogs, separated from them, howling on the riverbank. While he harbored plenty of his own aristocratic prejudices, he decried the hypocrisy of white Americans professing the ideals of democracy while forcing Native Americans and black Americans— in both slave-owning and supposedly "free" states—to live under tyranny. He predicted, sagely, that the evils of slavery would likely lead the nation into a civil war.

In addition, he saw another contradiction that he worried might portend the unraveling of the world's first major democracy. While Americans proudly proclaimed their liberties—their freedom to think and say anything and to associate with whomever they chose—they exercised, by Tocqueville's reckoning, very little *freedom of thought*. In America, he observed, the average person finds it "extremely difficult to believe what the bulk of the people reject, or to profess what they condemn."

In an observation that foreshadowed William Whyte's essay on groupthink in the 1950s, colleges exploding in protest over controversial authors being invited to speak on campus, and studies revealing people's inability to develop opinions contrary to their ideological tribes, Tocqueville wrote that "In America, the majority raises very formidable barriers to the liberty of opinion: within these barriers an author may write whatever he pleases, but he will repent it if he ever steps beyond them." As a result, he observed that "I know no country in which there is so little true independence of mind and freedom of discussion as in America."

In fact, for Tocqueville the "dangers which threaten the American union do not originate in diversity of interests or of opinions," but rather in "uniformity of thought" through which a "tyranny of the majority" could do far more to diminish personal freedoms than any monarch might aspire to do. "The authority of a king is purely physical," he noted, "and it controls the actions of the subject without subduing his private will; but the majority possesses a power which is physical and moral at the same time; it acts upon the will as well as upon the actions of men, and it represses not only all contest, but all controversy."

How democracy fades

The man in the White House at the time of Tocqueville's journey to America was Andrew Jackson, a populist rabble rouser who had, among other things, pushed the Indian Removal Act through Congress in 1830 (which led to the displacement of 125,000 native people) and had dismantled the national bank (which in turn, led to an economic depression). Tocqueville believed he had seen the worst impulses and outcomes of democracy—and its potential unraveling—made manifest. Jackson, in his view, was a "slave of the majority: he yields to its wishes, its propensities, and its demands" and panders to its whims and vagaries. After meeting Jackson, Tocqueville concluded that he was a "man of violent temper and very moderate talents; nothing in his whole career ever proved him qualified to govern a free people." Yet because the public was on his side, he was able to "trample on his personal enemies whenever they cross his path."[1]

In Tocqueville's view, Jackson reflected the worst aspects of small-minded political parties—driven by petty causes, strong personalities, and stirring people's emotions with hyperbolic language to secure their votes. In contrast, "great" parties, by his reckoning, reflected loftier principles, "generous passions" and "genuine convictions," and engaged in important debates. By the early 1830s, America's "great" parties had faded, replaced by two new parties (Democrats and Republicans), who were consumed with what Tocqueville viewed as "lesser controversies" (they mostly ignored slavery) that to a foreigner seemed "so incomprehensible and so puerile that he is at a loss whether to pity a people which takes such arrant trifles in good earnest, or to envy the happiness which enables it to discuss them."

Keeping the despots at bay

Yet not all hope was lost. One bulwark against America becoming a "despotic democracy," Tocqueville reasoned, was its free and independent newspapers. While he found most of them to be shoddily written and superficial (devoting three-quarters of their pages to ads and the rest to "trivial anecdotes" with few "passionate discussions" of the issues of the day) they were nonetheless common in every village. The sheer volume and number of publications in America was staggering, which meant people had access to a free flow of information which they could use to form their opinions. As Thomas Jefferson famously wrote in a letter to Edward Carrington, "were it left to me to decide whether we should have a government without newspapers or newspapers without a government, I should not hesitate a moment to prefer the latter. But I should mean that every man should receive those papers and be capable of reading them."

Of course, going from being capable of reading to developing well-informed opinions is hardly ever a straight line, given that most people, by Tocqueville's estimation, were "as apt to cling to their opinions from pride as from conviction." Again, with uncanny clairvoyance—or perhaps astute insight into human nature—Tocqueville forecasted a key challenge to sustaining a strong democracy.

Bolstering democracy with curiosity

Because he had seen democracy falter in his native France and America's own democracy was still relatively young (just over 50 years old), for Tocqueville, the question of how democracies flourish was hardly an academic one. Nor should we take our own democracy for granted. Worldwide, in fact, the rapid spread of democracy over the past two centuries has stalled in recent years with once democratic nations like Turkey, Hungary, Poland, Ukraine, and Venezuela sliding backwards into authoritarianism. According to a European Union-funded report tracking the progress of democracies in 170 nations from 1900 to 2016, democracies—that is, countries with open elections, laws to protect civil liberties, and constraints on executive power—have regressed to where they were 10 to 15 years ago.[2]

Consider, for example, China, which was once hailed as moving toward a freer, more democratic society. Recently, President Xi Jinping consolidated power and strong-armed the National People's Congress into removing his term limits, making him dictator for life. In Russia, Vladimir Putin's staunchest critics have died under suspicious circumstances[3] and he runs unopposed in staged elections. Overall, nearly a quarter of the world's population lives in countries without free and fair elections.

Meanwhile, even in stable democracies, including in the United States, a growing percentage of citizens (especially younger ones) have lost faith in democratic institutions. In the U.S., for example, 91 percent of people who were born in the 1930s say that it's "very important" for them to live in a country that is governed democratically, versus 57.1 percent of citizens born in the 1980s.[4]

Although the EU-funded report offered the reassurance that "alarmist reports about the global demise of democracy are unwarranted," it did note that "we may be at a watershed for democracy" given the declining faith in democratic institutions among people in established democracies, the erosion of democratic institutions if not outright relapses into autocracy in newer democracies, and increasing repression in less democratic nations, which all "suggest a global challenge to, and perhaps the future demise of, democracy."

What this all suggests is we cannot put our democracy on autopilot and expect it to stay aloft. Rather, we must engage in high-effort thinking often and long enough to choose candidates wisely, voice our opinions to elected officials, and keep those in office who actually govern well. Sustaining such thinking for long periods of time is not always easy to do—our brains are always more comfortable sliding back into groupthink and confirmation bias. Yet as we'll see in the next chapter, there is a way forward that can bring people together and also avoid the "soft despotism" of the tyranny of the majority. Once again, as you might imagine, that way forward starts with curiosity. 💡

CHAPTER EIGHTEEN

A Curious Bridge Across the Divide

Here's some good news: *Not everyone* succumbs so easily to politically motivated reasoning. In his study for science filmmakers that arrived at surprising insights about political thinking, Yale University's Dan Kahan and his colleagues found a small group of people who demonstrated a consistent ability to think outside their partisan boxes and form an opinion that, while perhaps not smack dab in the middle, was at least closer to other side's view—close enough, we might imagine, that they could reach across the gap, shake hands, and find consensus.[1]

So, who were these people?

Contrary to what you might think, they weren't what some partisans call dead armadillos (because they're found in the middle of the road). Rather, they included both *conservatives* and *liberals* who shared a special disposition: something called *scientific curiosity*. More precisely, they were the kind of people who were inclined to seek out new ideas no matter where they might lead—even if it created cognitive dissonance for them.

For example, when asked to pick from two factual news stories that most interested them, curious people who *believed* in climate change were more likely to choose to read an article that contradicted their preconceived ideas (e.g., "Scientists Find Still More Evidence that Global Warming Actually *Slowed* in Last Decade"). Similarly, curious people who were *skeptical* about climate change were more apt choose an article that contradicted their views (e.g., "Scientists Report Surprising Evidence: Arctic Ice Melting Faster Than Expected"). These highly curious people sought information that might *disconfirm* their biases in order "to experience the intrinsic pleasure of awe and surprise." They didn't mind having their intellectual bubbles burst, but instead, seemed to enjoy stretching their thinking.

As noted earlier, when researchers mapped people's levels of concern about global warming or fracking (from "extremely high risk" to "none at all") according to their *scientific knowledge*, they found increasingly divergent views—a sort of sideways V with liberal Democrats expressing increasing alarm and conservative Republicans expressing decreasing alarm as both groups moved to the 99th percentile of scientific knowledge.

However, when they mapped people's views according to scientific *curiosity*, they found a different pattern: two parallel lines gently sloping upward, with more curious conservatives expressing more, not less, concern about both issues.

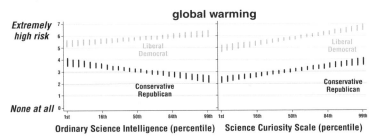

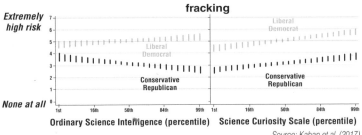

Source: Kahan et al. (2017)

In short, the researchers found that scientific curiosity appeared to *counteract* the effects of politically motivated reasoning.

Curiously less divided

A recent study appears to suggest that curiosity may, in fact, help to bridge ideological divides and help us find middle ground even on hot-button issues. Recently, researchers at the University of Illinois at Urbana-Champaign asked 174 college students for their opinions on a politically dicey topic: whether a mosque should be built near the Ground Zero site in New York City, something they knew from earlier research tended to divide people, with liberals favoring and conservatives opposing the idea.[2] However, before asking for their opinions, the researchers first split the students into two randomly assigned groups and invited them to engage in starkly different mental exercises. The first group responded to a series of pragmatic *how-to* questions about mental health, starting with "How would you improve and maintain mental health?" followed by three additional *how* questions. The second group responded to a series of self-reflective *why* questions, starting with "Why would I improve and maintain mental health?" followed by three subsequent *why* questions.

Afterward, the researchers showed students three pictures related to the 9/11 attacks, had them read about the plan to build a mosque near Ground Zero, and then asked them to share whether they viewed the proposal to build the mosque negatively or positively. Students who engaged in the *concrete* thinking exercise demonstrated much the same pattern in their responses as the general population: Self-identified liberals strongly favored the mosque and self-identified conservatives strongly opposed it. No surprise there.

However, students who had engaged in the *abstract* thinking exercise beforehand offered more-similar, and more-neutral, responses to the proposed mosque despite their politically divergent starting points. Basically, priming students' brains with reflective thinking via simple *why* questions—what we might call *curiosity thinking*—seemed to tamp down more extreme positions, moving respondents beyond their ideological bubbles and toward a middle ground in their thinking.

United in curiosity

So, could curiosity help to heal our political divide and keep our democracy healthy? Hopefully, yes, especially when we consider its demonstrated links with compassion and better interpersonal relationships. As we've seen, not only does curiosity prompt our exploration of the world around us, but also our willingness to connect with others and appreciate their perspectives.

Perhaps even more important, as we learned in the previous section, when groups face complex challenges, they must employ both "big picture" curiosity to "zoom out" and see larger trends in the changing world, and introspective curiosity to "zoom in" to remind themselves of *what* worked in the past and *why* it worked—in short, recalling and renewing shared values and principles.

In theory, these two impulses would seem to be complementary—balancing the need to change with the times while holding fast to core values. In practice, though, the existence of these two types of thinking is often the very thing that most divides liberals from conservatives: Most Democrats (68 percent) believe the nation's success lies in its "ability to change" whereas most Republicans (61 percent) say it lies in our "reliance on long-standing principles."[3]

A curious balancing act

If Alexis de Tocqueville were alive today, he'd likely say both sides are right—they represent two sides of the same coin, of a free and democratic society. During his travels across America, he admired how readily Americans faced the future: their optimism, inventiveness, and willingness to overturn convention. In fact, it was Americans' willingness to take up new ideas and shake up old ways of doing things that prompted him to conclude that the nation—as grubby and provincial as it was back in 1831, with pigs still roaming the streets of New York City—would one day be a great nation. On the other hand, he also admired how rooted the nation was in deeply (and often religiously) held principles of freedom, equality, and charity.

The productive tension in any free society, he surmised, lay in striking the right balance between the two guiding principles—freedom and equality—that are embedded in the opening lines of the Declaration of Independence:

> We hold these truths to be self-evident, that all Men are created equal, that they are endowed by their Creator with certain unalienable Rights, that among these are Life, Liberty, and the Pursuit of Happiness.

In practice, of course, balancing these ideals—individual liberties with equal rights—is never easy. That's because one person's freedoms are always bounded by others' rights—the "freedom" to dump toxic sludge into a river impedes the rights of others to drink clean water or catch fish downstream. So, too, ensuring equality for one group often means telling another group they are no longer "free" to do as they choose—like excluding certain groups of people from buying or renting property. In Tocqueville's estimation, swinging the pendulum too far toward individual freedom can lead to gross inequalities and survival-of-the-fittest anarchy; swinging it too far toward equality could lead to suffocating homogeneity and authoritarianism. Thus, democracies must continually negotiate the balance between these principles of freedom and equality. For Tocqueville, such questions were the domain of "great" political parties that rose above petty bickering and kept political discourse focused on the deeper *whys* of a nation's guiding principles and shared values. Such issues are rarely easily settled; they're often quite contentious, but eminently worth debating.

Modern writer Simon Sinek notes that great leaders throughout history have started not with *what*, but with *why*. Martin Luther King, Jr., for example, inspired people not with the *what* and *how* of civil rights—he didn't fill his speeches with facts or arcane policy details—but rather, with the *why*—namely, when a society's laws conflict with higher law, society must change its laws. By helping people see the values they shared, Dr. King was able to grow a larger movement that drew both white and black people together, united with a shared sense of purpose and understanding that if one of our fellow Americans is debased, we as a nation are debased.

Finding a way forward . . . together

So, where do we go from here? How might we convert curiosity into better political understanding and discourse? Here are a few ideas to consider.

Musing #1: Read more, watch less.

The very format of modern cable news would appear to impede our ability to arrive at our own judgments about issues of the day. That's because cable networks have become increasingly slanted toward either liberals or conservatives, or they pit dueling ideologues against one another seemingly for sport. However, as the study of Yale students demonstrates, learning what members of our own (or an opposing) ideological group thinks about hot-button issues tends to trigger politically motivated reasoning versus simply learning about an issue, or thinking more deeply about it, sans commentary. Not so long ago, most of us consumed TV news via a more straightforward presentation of information: Tom Brokaw, Dan Rather, or Peter Jennings would report *without* commentary because, per FCC regulations, doing so would trigger "equal time" provisions. Nowadays, though, the most widely watched news shows on cable are those that process information via commentators, not news anchors. On top of that, most 24-hour news channels flit frenetically from one issue to the next—tax cuts, hurricanes, gun control, trade wars, sexual harassment, nuclear threats, the list goes on and on—without giving viewers the opportunity to engage in *scientific curiosity* about these topics or helping them to consider deeper, more reflective *why* questions.

So, what are we to do? Well, you might start with what you're doing right now: reading actual words in whole sentences, not Twitter or Facebook feeds. Books, magazines, and newspapers let us be more self-directed in our learning, which, after all is the very heart of curiosity. Newspapers, for example, cover between 70 and 100 stories per day, whereas we can listen to a half-hour news broadcast and encounter only about 15 stories.[4] Thus, when we *read*, rather than *watch*, we become more active and curious consumers of information.

Musing #2: Be politically and compassionately curious.

It's normal to be reluctant to engage in a political conversation with others for fear of angering them or becoming angry ourselves. Yet such reluctance may reflect that we're going about political discourse all wrong—as a *debate*, not a *dialogue*. If we see political conversations as a debate, we often quickly find ourselves in an unproductive, ideological cage match, like this:

> "I can't believe you think it's OK for people to own those weapons!"

> "Well, I can't believe you're OK with tearing up the Second Amendment!"

But if we recognize that facts alone rarely change anyone's opinion—and that our opinions are largely shaped by what we *feel* and *value*—we might see that the purpose of political dialogue isn't to persuade or dissuade, but rather to *appreciate* one another and in so doing, perhaps find some common ground. We might even borrow some of Arthur and Elaine Aron's 36 questions that were designed to bring people together to talk about their *aspirations* and *values*, share *what they like about* one another, and ultimately, find common ground in *shared connections* and mutual *problem solving*. If we could engage one another in appreciative inquiry, one that starts with what we like about each other and begins to surface shared values, we might actually get somewhere, like this:

> "I know we both want to protect our families and to live in a free and safe neighborhood. So, help me understand how making guns so available makes you feel safer, because it makes me feel less safe."

> "Well, I want to protect my own home. Knowing I can defend my family makes me feel safer. It's also a bigger picture thing: I'm afraid if the government took away our guns, a dictator could take us over."

> "That's interesting. You're talking about freedom and safety in a larger democratic sense, while I've been thinking about it in more of day-to-day sense of feeling safe at the mall, the movie theater,

or school. So, it makes me sad—and mad—to see those images of shootings on TV."

"I feel both of those things, too. I also don't like seeing dangerous weapons get into the hands of mentally ill people. Still, I worry about someone in the government saying who can and cannot have a gun."

"So, maybe somewhere between anarchy and totalitarianism there's a solution. I'll bet if we got enough reasonable people together—like us—we could probably find a reasonable solution."

"Yeah, I'll bet you're right. We both want the same things—freedom and safety. Maybe we just need to calm down the rhetoric a bit and talk things through."

Such dialogues, of course, won't resolve contentious issues overnight, but if more and more of us—and our policymakers—had them, we might see there is far more that brings us together than divides us. And if nothing else, our backyard barbecues with neighbors could be less tense and more enjoyable.

Musing #3: Seeing beyond "partyism."

While partisanship is nothing new (Tocqueville observed it way back in the 1830s), the current level of "partyism" is likely not good for our society, or for us as individuals, notes columnist David Brooks. "There is a tremendous variety of human beings within each political party," he notes, so "to judge human beings on political labels is to deny and ignore what is most important about them. It is to profoundly devalue them. That is the core sin of prejudice, whether it is racism or partyism."[5] Brooks urges everyone to burst their own ideological bubbles from time to time—to understand, for example, that the "truth is plural. There is no one, correct answer to the big political questions" of the day.

Moreover, we should all recognize that politics is a limited activity—government can help keep us safe and grant us the liberty to pursue happiness, but ultimately, we do that ourselves through "loving relationships, thick communities and wise friends."[6] Perhaps most important, like any good leader, we need the courage and humility to recognize that we don't have all the answers. If we can do that, we can *moderate* our views and find ways to come together, across the divide. "Moderation requires courage," Brooks adds. "Moderates don't operate from the safety of their ideologically pure galleons. They are unafraid to face the cross currents, detached from clan, acknowledging how little they know." Acknowledging how little we know, of course, is the beginning of curiosity.

Musing #4: Respectfully agreeing to disagree.

Recently, a group called Better Angels brought small groups of a dozen or so people from both sides of the political divide together to show them how to engage in cool-headed, thoughtful dialogue with one another on a series of hot-button issues like gun control. Initially, sitting in like-minded groups, people shared the stereotypes they figured people on the other side of the divide held about them.

Liberals, for example, assumed that conservatives believed them to be unpatriotic, fiscally irresponsible, and wishy-washy on crime. Conservatives, meanwhile, figured liberals pegged them as racist, uneducated, and greedy. Afterward, the two groups came together to share what they thought was *really* true about themselves. Next, they sat in a "fishbowl" with an inner circle facing the outer circle and took turns sharing their values and why they believed their policy prescriptions were better for the country. Finally, they provided a self-critique of the shortcomings of their own respective sides.

By the end of the evening, people on both sides came to realize they had more in common with one another than news broadcasts had led them to believe. "To actually achieve an honest disagreement, to see what areas you agree and disagree on and what common ground you can find, you can't do it just by watching MSNBC or Fox News," observed David Blankenhorn, one of the group's founders. "You have to put a little effort into it, and it involves interacting with people on the other side."[7]

The purpose of such dialogue isn't to come to consensus, of course. Most people don't change their views about policy issues or what they value, but they do begin to change their views of *people on the other side of the divide*, often realizing that they value the same things—freedom, equality, justice—and that they are also trying to work out the proper balance among them.

Years ago, when policymakers in Finland set out to reform their education system and in turn grow their economy, they tapped into a deeply held, shared cultural value, something the Finns call *sisu*—a term that describes a sort of rugged determination to never give up and to act rationally in the face of adversity.[8] Tapping into this value—Finns' deep reservoir of pride and resilience—gave them the deep *why* they needed to transform their education system into one of the most respected in the world.

The writings of Alexis de Tocqueville show us that like the Finns' ethos of *sisu*, the roots of curiosity and compassion run deep in our nation and are made manifest in our ingenuity, optimism, and ability to pull together to solve big challenges. We'd do well to remember that it's not simply "amber waves of grain" or "purple mountain majesties" that have attracted generations of newcomers to America since the early years of the nation, but these curiosity-fueled values.

Nor do we need to look far to see curiosity in our national character and history. We can see it in Benjamin Franklin flying a kite in a thunderstorm, George Washington Carver transforming the lowly peanut into more than 300 products, the Wright Brothers flying the first plane at Kitty Hawk, and Neil Armstrong stepping onto the moon. And we see it in the courageous curiosity of people like Frederick Douglass, Susan B. Anthony, and Rosa Parks who didn't accept our society as it was, but rather saw it through the lens of its unfulfilled promises and kept asking *what if* questions. By embracing our collective curiosity and continuing to ask questions about who we are and hope to be as a nation we may continue to reflect what Tocqueville most admired about the young, imperfect nation he visited. "The greatness of America," he wrote, "lies not in being more enlightened than any other nation, but rather in her ability to repair her faults."

Standing at a Curious Crossroads

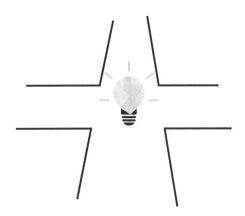

"Don't let anyone rob you of your imagination, your creativity, or your curiosity. It's your place in the world; it's your life. Go on and do all you can with it, and make it the life you want to live."

–Mae Jemison

Standing at a Curious Crossroads

We're all born curious. It's what makes us human—the desire to explore, to learn, and to connect with other people. It's deeply embedded in all of us. As we've seen, it's also something that's quintessentially American, something evident from the nation's earliest days and in generation after generation of starry-eyed wonderers and wanderers who kept envisioning—and helping others to envision—a more perfect union and a better future for all our citizens.

Yet some of our present troubles suggest we may be running out of curiosity, as individuals, a society, and a nation. For example,

◊ Twenty years of heavy-handed reforms narrowly focused on standardized achievement tests have left many students disengaged and educators dispirited—that is, feeling *incurious*.

◊ Authentic interpersonal bonds have withered in our digitally connected, "alone together" society. Depression, drug addictions, and alcohol abuse are all on the rise, for reasons that appear to include people lacking interpersonal connections and meaning in their lives.

◊ Although the U.S. continues to lead the world in patent seeking, its share of the world's patents has fallen, leading to concern that we may be losing our edge in innovation—due in part to public and private investment in R&D remaining relatively flat while other nations, most notably China, have dramatically increased, and quietly eclipsed, the U.S. in its R&D spending and output.[1]

◊ Our lack of interest in, and compassion for, others seems to have led to a boiling over of partisan animus and social tensions—whether it's coastal America ignoring the plight of people in "fly-over" country whose livelihoods have been decimated by globalization; wealthier Americans lacking inquisitiveness about the historic disenfranchisement of urban communities and minorities; companies and whole industries systematically ignoring and suppressing the voices of women facing sexual harassment; conservatives feeling stereotyped by liberals as racists, bigots, and "deplorables"; or liberals feeling stereotyped as out-of-touch, unpatriotic libertines or as "nasty women" who do not value personal responsibility.

We can change all of this, of course. All it would take is for everyone to rekindle our sense of wonder about other people and the world around us—and to help others do the same.

Imagine for a moment what it might look like if we did that—if we shifted our conversations in schools, workplaces, news feeds, and backyard barbecues from preconceived notions of *what's wrong* to open-minded, shared exploration of *what ifs*. Imagine what new possibilities for the future might spring *out of curiosity*. For instance, we might:

◊ Reimagine our schools as places that let students develop their *intellectual curiosity* to become scientists, entrepreneurs, inventors, caregivers, and real-world problem solvers who cultivate *interpersonal curiosity* to become compassionate citizens who seek to understand one another, solve problems together, and give back to their communities. By helping our youth become *curious people*, we might help them find greater purpose and meaning in their lives.

◊ Put down our phones and just talk to one another—no tweets, no likes, no pins—considering meaningful questions that go beyond the superficial and delve into deeper places where we find real connections. In so doing, we might begin to appreciate one another in new ways and find there's far more that unites than divides us.

◊ Fixate less on pursuing happiness (and material goods), which only make us more miserable, and realize that instead, we can find joy in wondering and wandering, especially when our wandering leads us back to what matters most—connecting deeply with others.

◊ Create companies and organizations that help everyone experience the joy of tapping into their own curiosity to create everyday innovations, discover better ways of working together, create more energetic enterprises, and get a little better, every day, at what we do.

◊ Occasionally pop our own ideological bubbles to appreciate others' views and find ways to meet in the middle—or at the very least, harbor less fear and loathing of those on the other side. Doing so might lead us to a shared understanding that while democracy is always messy and we as a nation will always be a fractious flotilla, we can still sail in the same general direction with our sextants focused on the stars of freedom and fairness.

By the same token, curiosity need not be so grandiose; it can also be quite simple and personal, bubbling up from within us. Yes, people can trigger or stifle our curiosity, but ultimately, being curious is a choice we can make every day for ourselves.

We can wake up and decide we already know everything there is to know, that we have all the right answers, and there's nothing new to experience, no one new to meet, no new places to go, and no new discoveries to make. In short, we can decide to live a life of no surprises—hemmed in by the familiar, the certain, and the ordinary. That is, we can choose to be *incurious*—living a humdrum, predictable existence in the shadowed vale of what we already know, or think we know.

Or, we can decide that today and every day after, we hope to wake up curious, priming our brains for learning and opening our minds to new possibilities. We can decide to search for new answers, explore new places (even if it's just a different street on our way home from work), and get to know one person a little better. We can emerge from the shadows of the predictable, mundane, and familiar, climb a hill and search for something that lies just beyond our horizon—be it physical, intellectual, interpersonal, or introspective.

In short, we all can decide whether we wish to *run out of curiosity*, letting it fade from our lives like a forgotten childhood friend, or we can decide to keep asking questions, exploring new places, searching for new answers, and making new connections . . . *out of curiosity*.

In the end, that may be the most important and encouraging thing about curiosity: It's within each of us, waiting to be developed. Although others may attempt to suppress our curiosity, it's still there, like a cork held underwater, waiting to pop back to the surface as soon as we release it again. Being a curious person need not be a chore or something we work assiduously to develop, but rather, something we do in small and simple ways, following one question after another, like a string of lamps lighting our way through the darkness.

So, with that in mind, I leave you to wonder and wander with one final question: What are you curious about now? 💡

References

Prologue

[1] Swan, G. E., & Carmelli, D. (1996). Curiosity and mortality in aging adults: A 5-year follow-up of the western collaborative group study. *Psychology and Aging, 11*(3), 449–453.

[2] Hsee, C. K., & Ruan, B. (2016). The Pandora effect: The power and peril of curiosity. *Psychological Science, 27*(5), 659–666.

[3] Bronson, P., & Merryman, A. (2010, July 10). The creativity crisis. *Newsweek.* Retrieved from www.newsweek.com/2010/07/10/the-creativity-crisis.html

Chapter 1

[1, 4, 7, 8, 9] Loewenstein, G. (1994). The psychology of curiosity: A review and reinterpretation. *Psychology Bulletin, 116*(1), 75–98.

[2, 3, 5, 6] Engel, S. (2015). *The hungry mind: The origins of curiosity in childhood.* Cambridge, MA: Harvard University Press.

[10] Lowry, N., & Johnson, D. W. (1981). Effects of controversy on epistemic curiosity, achievement, and attitudes. *Journal of Social Psychology, 115*, 31–43.

[11] Kashdan, T., Stiksma, M. C., Disabato, D. J., McKnight, P. E., Bekier, J., Kaji, J., & Lazarus, R. (2018). The five-dimensional curiosity scale: Capturing the bandwidth of curiosity and identifying four unique subgroups of curious people. *Journal of Research in Personality, 73*, 130–149.

Chapter 2

[1] Gaffigan, J. (2013). *Dad is fat* (pp. 117–118). New York: Three Rivers Press.

[2] Medina, J. (2008). *Brain rules: 12 principles for surviving and thriving at work, home, and school.* Seattle, WA: Pear Press.

[3] Raine, A., Reynolds, C., Venables, P. H., & Mednick, S. A. (2002). Stimulation seeking and intelligence: A prospective longitudinal study. *Journal of Personality and Social Psychology, 82*(4), 663–674.

[4] Grossmann, K. E., Grossmann, K., Huber, F. & Wartner, U. (1981). German children's behavior towards their mothers at 12 months and their fathers at 18 months in Ainsworth's Strange Situation. *International Journal of Behavioral Development, 4*, 157–181.

[5] Campos, J. J., Barrett, K. C., Lamb, M. E., Goldsmith, H. H., & Stenberg, C. (1983). Socioemotional development. In M. M. Haith & J. J. Campos (Eds.), *Handbook of child psychology (Vol. 2): Infancy and developmental psychobiology.* New York: Wiley.

[6] Durkin, K. (1995). *Developmental social psychology: From infancy to old age.* Malden, MA: Blackwell Publishing.

[7] Vaughn, B., Lefever, G. B., Seifer, R., & Barglow, P. (1989). Attachment behavior, attachment security, and temperament during infancy. *Child Development, 60,* 728–737.

[8] Moore, S. G., & Bulbulian, K. N. (1976). The effects of contrasting styles of adult-child interaction on children's curiosity. *Developmental Psychology, 12*(2), 171–172.

[9] Henderson, B. & Moore, S. G. (1980). Children's responses to objects differing in novelty in relation to level of curiosity and adult behavior. *Child Development, 51*(2), 457–465.

[10] Van Schijndel, T. J. P., Franse, R. K., & Raijmakers, M. E. J. (2010). The exploratory behavior scale: Assessing young visitors' hands-on behavior in science museums. *Science Education, 94*(5), 794–809.

[11] Engel, S. (2015). *The hungry mind: The origins of curiosity in childhood.* Cambridge, MA: Harvard University Press.

[12] Hackmann, H., & Engel, S. (2002). *Curiosity in context: The classroom environment examined.* Unpublished honors thesis. Williams College, Williamstown, MA (p. 635).

[13] Goertzel, T. (2004). Cradles of eminence—then and now. *Parenting for High Potential.* Retrieved from https://www.questia.com/magazine/1P3-741068721/cradles-of-eminence-then-and-now

[14] Goertzel, V., Goertzel, M. G., Goertzel, T. G., & Hansen, A. (2004). *Cradles of eminence: Childhoods of more than 700 famous men and women.* Tucson, AZ: Gifted Psychology Press.

Chapter 3

[1] Aron, A. R., Shohamy, D., Clark, J., Myers, C., Gluck, M. A., & Poldrack, R. A. (2004). Human midbrain sensitivity to cognitive feedback and uncertainty during classification learning. *Journal of Neurophysiology, 92*(2), 1144–1152.

[2] Gruber, M. J., Gelman, B. D., & Ranganath, C. (2014). States of curiosity modulate hippocampus-dependent learning via the dopaminergic circuit. *Neuron, 84*(2), 486–496.

[3] Stanovich, K. E. (1986). Matthew effects in reading: Some consequences of individual differences in the acquisition of literacy. *Reading Research Quarterly, 21*(4), 360–406.

[4] Heshmat, S. (2015, January 22). The addictive quality of curiosity: Curiosity as an antidote to boredom and addiction [blog post]. *Psychology Today.* Retrieved from https://www.psychologytoday.com/blog/science-choice/201501/the-addictive-quality-curiosity

Chapter 4

[1] Gottfried, A. E., Fleming, J., & Gottfried, A. W. (2001). Continuity of academic intrinsic motivation from childhood through late adolescence: A longitudinal study. *Journal of Educational Psychology, 93*(1), 3–13.

[2, 3, 4] Csikszentmihalyi, M., Rathunde, K., & Whalen, S. (1993). *Talented teenagers: The roots of success & failure.* New York: Cambridge University Press.

[5] Torrance, P. E. (1963). The creativity personality and the ideal pupil. *Teachers College Record, 3*, 220–226.

[6] Torrance, P. E. (1965). *Rewarding creative behavior: Experiments in classroom creative behavior.* Englewood Cliffs, NJ: Prentice Hall.

[7] Engelhard, G. (1985). *The discovery of educational goals and outcomes: A view of the latent curriculum of schooling.* Unpublished doctoral dissertation. University of Chicago, Chicago, IL.

[8] Engelhard, G., & Monsaas, J. A. (1988). Grade level, gender and school-related curiosity in urban elementary schools. *Journal of Educational Research, 82*(1), 22–26.

[9, 10] Engel, S. (2011). Children's need to know: Curiosity in schools. *Harvard Educational Review, 81*(4), 625–645.

[11] Yazzie-Mintz, E. (2010). *Charting the path from engagement to achievement: A report on the 2009 High School Survey of Student Engagement.* Bloomington, IN: Center for Evaluation & Education.

[12, 13] Stigler, J. W., & Hiebert, J. (2004). Improving mathematics teaching. *Educational Leadership, 61*(5), 12–17.

[14] Medina, J. (2008). *Brain rules* (p. 5). Seattle, WA: Pear Tree Press.

[15] IHI Multimedia Team. (2015). Like Magic? ("Every system is perfectly designed…") [Blog]. Retrieved from http://www.ihi.org/communities/blogs/origin-of-every-system-is-perfectly-designed-quote

Chapter 5

[1] National Commission on Excellence in Education. (1983, April). *A nation at risk: The imperative for educational reform.* Retrieved from https://www2.ed.gov/pubs/NatAtRisk/index.html

[2] Berliner, D. C., & Biddle, B. J. (1995). *The manufactured crisis: Myths, fraud, and the attack on America's public schools.* Reading, MA: Addison-Wesley.

[3] Carson, C. C., Huelskamp, R. M., & Woodall, T. D. (1992). Perspectives on education in America: An annotated briefing. *The Journal of Educational Research, 86*(5), 259–265, 267–291, 293–297, 299–307, 309–310.

[4] Marzano, R., & Kendall, J. (1998). *Awash in a sea of standards.* Denver, CO: McREL.

[5] Lazarín, M. (2014). *Testing overload in America's schools.* Washington, DC: Center for American Progress.

[6] Winerip, M. (2011, March 6). Evaluating New York teachers: Perhaps the numbers do lie. *The New York Times.* Retrieved from https://www.nytimes.com/2011/03/07/education/07winerip.html

[7] Schochet, P. Z., & Chiang, H. S. (2010). *Error rates in measuring teacher and school performance based on student test score gains (NCEE 2010-4004).* Washington, DC: National Center for Education Evaluation and Regional Assistance, Institute of Education Sciences, U.S. Department of Education.

[8] Clawson, L. (2012, March 4). New York City's flawed data fuel right's war on teachers. *Daily Kos.* Retrieved from www.dailykos.com/story/2012/30/04/1069927/-New-York-City-s-flawed-data-fuels-the-right-s-war-on-teachers

[9] Metlife. (2013). *The MetLife survey of the American teacher: Challenges of school leadership.* Retrieved from https://www.metlife.com/assets/cao/foundation/Met Life-Teacher-Survey-2012.pdf

[10] Strauss, V. (2015, June 12). Why so many teachers leave—and how to get them to stay. *The Washington Post.* Retrieved from https://www.washingtonpost.com/news/answer-sheet/wp/2015/06/12/why-so-many-teachers-leave-and-how-to-get-them-to-stay/?utm_term=.f701f59b92f3

[11] Bridgeland, J. M., DiIulio, J., & Morison, K. B. (2006). *The silent epidemic: Perspectives of high school dropouts.* Washington, DC: Civic Enterprises.

[12] Smith, T. (2014, March 17). Does teaching kids to get 'gritty' help them get ahead? [Radio broadcast]. *National Public Radio.* Retrieved from http://www.npr.org/sections/ed/2014/03/17/290089998/does-teaching-kids-to-get-gritty-help-them-get-ahead

[13] Goodwin, B. (2015). Getting unstuck. *Educational Leadership, 72,* 8–12.

[14] Goodman, J. (2012). *Gold standards? State standards reform and student achievement.* Cambridge, MA: Program on Education Policy and Governance, Harvard University. Retrieved from www.hks.harvard.edu/pepg/PDF/Papers/PEPG12-05

[15] Pianta, R. C., Belsky, J., Houts, R., & Morrison, F. (2007). Opportunities to learn in America's elementary classrooms. *Science, 315*(5820), 1795–1796.

[16, 18] Organisation for Economic Cooperation and Development (OECD). (2011). *Strong performers and successful reformers in education: Lessons from PISA for the United States.* Retrieved from www.oecd.org/dataoecd/32/50/46623978.pdf

[17] Sahlberg, P. (2012). *Finnish lessons: What can the world learn from educational change in Finland?* New York: Teachers' College Press.

[19] Levitt, S. D., List, J. A., Neckerman, S., & Sadoff, S. (2012). The behavioralist goes to school: Leveraging behavioral economics to improve educational

performance (*NBER Working Paper Series* No. 18165). Cambridge, MA: National Bureau of Economic Research.

[20] Warren, T. (2013, November 12). Microsoft axes its controversial employee ranking system [blog post]. *The Verge*. Retrieved from www.theverge.com/2013/11/12/5094864/microsoft-kills-stack-ranking-internal-structure

[21] Deutschman, A. (2006). *Change or die: Three keys to change at work and in life.* New York: HarperBusiness; Pink, D. H. (2009). *Drive: The surprising truth about what motivates us.* New York: Riverhead Books; Sinek, S. (2011). *Start with why.* New York: Portfolio.

[22] Engel, S. (2015). *The hungry mind: The origins of curiosity in childhood* (p. 636). Cambridge, MA: Harvard University Press.

[23] Csikszentmihalyi, M., Rathunde, K., & Whalen, S. (1993). *Talented teenagers: The roots of success & failure.* New York: Cambridge University Press.

[24] Gottfried, A. E., Fleming, J., & Gottfried, A. W. (2001). Continuity of academic intrinsic motivation from childhood through late adolescence: A longitudinal study. *Journal of Educational Psychology, 93*(1), 3–13.

[25] Engel, S., & Randall, K. (2009). How teachers respond to children's inquiry. *American Educational Research Journal, 46*(1), 183–202.

Chapter 6

[1] Engel, S. (2015). *The hungry mind: The origins of curiosity in childhood.* Cambridge, MA: Harvard University Press.

[2] Goodwin, B. (2003, December). *Digging deeper: Where does the public stand on standards-based education?* Aurora, CO: Mid-continent Research for Education and Learning (McREL).

[3] Cushman, K. (2010). *Fires in the mind: What kids can tell us about motivation and mastery.* San Francisco: Jossey-Bass.

[4] Larson, L. R., & Lovelace, M. D. (2013). Evaluating the efficacy of questioning strategies in lecture-based classroom environments: Are we asking the right questions? *Journal on Excellence in College Teaching, 24*(1), 105–122.

[5] Munro, J. (2015). *Curiouser and curiouser* (p. 10). Denver, CO: McREL International.

[6] Jones, M. G. (1990). Action zone theory, target students and science classroom interactions. *Journal of Research in Science Teaching, 27*(8), 651–660.

[7] Walsh, J. A., & Sattes, B. D. (2016). *Quality questioning: Research-based practice to engage every learner, 2ⁿᵈ Ed.* Thousand Oaks, CA: Corwin.

[8] Maheady, L., Mallette, B., Harper, G. F., & Sacca, K. (1991). Heads together: A peer-mediated option for improving the academic achievement of heterogeneous learning groups. *Remedial and Special Education, 12*(2), 25–33.

[9] Kelly, S., & Turner, J. (2009). Rethinking the effects of classroom activity structure on the engagement of low-achieving students. *Teachers College Record, 111*(7), 1665–1692.

[10] Good, T. L., Slavings, R. L., Harel, K. H., & Emerson, H. (1987). Student passivity: A study of question asking in K–12 classrooms. *Sociology of Education, 60*, 181–199.

[11] Patall, E., Cooper, H., & Robinson, J. C. (2008). The effects of choice on intrinsic motivation and related outcomes: A meta-analysis of research findings. *Psychological Bulletin, 134*(2), 270–300.

[12] National Park Service. (n.d.). *The life of Theodore Roosevelt*. Retrieved from https://www.nps.gov/thri/theodorerooseveltbio.htm

[13] Isaacson, W. (2007). 20 things you need to know about Albert Einstein. *Time*. Retrieved from http://content.time.com/time/specials/packages/article/0,28804,1936731_1936743_1936745,00.html

[14] Williams, C. (2018). The perks of a play-in-the-mud educational philosophy. *The Atlantic*. Retrieved from https://www.theatlantic.com/education/archive/2018/04/early-childhood-outdoor-education/558959/

[15] Louv, R. (2008). *Last child in the woods: Saving our children from nature-deficit disorder*. Chapel Hill, NC: Algonquin Books.

[16] Taylor, A. F., Kuo, F. E., & Sullivan, W. C. (2001). *Environment and Behavior, 33*(1), 54–77.

[17] Barker, J. E., Semenov, A. D., Michaelson, L., Provan, L. S., Snyder, H. R., & Munakata, Y. (2014). Less-structured time in children's daily lives predicts self-directed executive functioning. *Frontiers in Psychology, 5*(593). Retrieved from https://www.frontiersin.org/articles/10.3389/fpsyg.2014.00593/full

[18] Friedman, T. L. (2005, April 3). It's a flat world, after all. *The New York Times*. Retrieved from www.nytimes.com/2005/04/03/magazine/its-a-flat-world-after-all.html?_r=0

[19] Hacker, A. (2012, July 29). Is algebra necessary? *The New York Times*. Retrieved from www.nytimes.com/2012/07/29/opinion/sunday/is-algebra-necessary.html

[20] Subotnik, R. F., Tai, R. H., & Almarode, J. (2011, May 10–12). *Study of the impact of selective SMT high schools: Reflections on learners gifted and motivated in science and mathematics*. Paper prepared for the workshop of the Committee on Highly Successful Schools or Programs for K–12 STEM Education, National Research Council, Washington, DC.

[21, 22, 23, 24] National Research Council. (2011). *Successful K-12 STEM education: Identifying effective approaches in science, technology, engineering, and mathematics* (p. 8). Washington, DC: The National Academies Press.

[25] Young, V. M., House, A., Wang, H., Singleton, C., & Klopfenstein, K. (2011). *Inclusive STEM schools: Early promise in Texas and unanswered questions.* Washington, DC: National Research Council.

[26] Tyre, P. (2016). The math revolution. *The Atlantic.* Retrieved from www.theatlantic.com/magazine/archive/2016/03/the-math-revolution/426855/

Chapter 7

[1] Black, J. S., & Gregersen, H. B. (2014). *It starts with one: Changing individuals changes organizations.* Upper Saddle River, NJ: Pearson Education, Inc.

[2] Carroll, P. B., & Mui, C. (2008). *Billion dollar lessons.* New York: Penguin Group.

[3,4] Satell, G. (2014, September 5). A look back at why Blockbuster really failed and why it didn't have to. *Forbes.* Retrieved from https://www.forbes.com/sites/gregsatell/2014/09/05/a-look-back-at-why-blockbuster-really-failed-and-why-it-didnt-have-to/#15127de41d64

[5,6] Kahneman, D. (2011). *Thinking fast and slow.* New York: Farrar, Straus & Giroux.

[7] Whyte, W. (1952). Groupthink. *Fortune.* Retrieved from http://fortune.com/2012/07/22/groupthink-fortune-1952/

[8] Bryk, A. S., Gomez, L. M., Grunow, A., & LeMahieu, P. (2015). *Learning to improve: How America's schools can get better at getting better* (p. 24). Cambridge, MA: Harvard Education Press.

[9] West, H. (2014, June 14). *A chain of innovation: The creation of Swiffer.* Retrieved from www.tmcnet.com/usubmit/2014/06/14/7876042.htm

[10,12] Collins, J. (2009). *How the mighty fall: And why some companies never give in.* New York: HarperCollins.

[11] Berenson, A., Harris, G., Meier, B., & Pollack, A. (2004, November 14). Despite warnings, drug giant took long path to Vioxx recall. *The New York Times.* Retrieved from http://www.nytimes.com/2004/11/14/business/despite-warnings-drug-giant-took-long-path-to-vioxx-recall.html

Chapter 8

[1] Reio, T. G., & Wiswell, A. (2000). Field investigation of the relationship among adult curiosity, workplace learning, and job performance. *Human Resource Development Quarterly, 11*(1), 5–30.

[2] Mussel, P. (2012). Introducing the construct curiosity for predicting job performance. *Journal of Organizational Behavior, 34,* 453–472.

[3] Celik, P., Storme, M., Davila, A., & Myszkowski, N. (2016). Work-related curiosity positively predicts worker innovation. *Journal of Management Development, 35*(9), 1184–1194.

[4] Collischon, M. (2017). *The returns to personality traits across the wage distribution.* Berlin: The German Socio-Economic Panel Study.

[5] Merck KGaA. (2016). *Be curious: The state of curiosity report.* Darmstadt, Germany: Author.

[6,7] Bessen, J. (2014, August 25). Employers aren't just whining—the "skills gap" is real. *Harvard Business Review.* Retrieved from https://hbr.org/2014/08/employers-arent-just-whining-the-skills-gap-is-real

[8] Labi, A. (2014). *Closing the skills gap: Companies and colleges collaborating for change.* Retrieved from www.luminafoundation.org/files/publications/Closing_the_skills_gap.pdf

[9] Minor, D., Brook, P., & Bernoff, J. (2017, December 28). Are innovative companies more profitable? MITSloan Management Review. [Blog]. Retrieved from https://sloanreview.mit.edu/article/are-innovative-companies-more-profitable/

[10] Peljko, Z. Jeraj, M., Săvoiu, G., & Marič, M. (2017). An empirical study of the relationship between entrepreneurial curiosity and innovativeness. *Organizacija, 49*(3), 172–182.

[11] Fernández-Aráoz, C. (2014). 21st century talent spotting. *Harvard Business Review, 92*(6), 46–56. Retrieved from https://hbr.org/2014/06/21st-century-talent-spotting

[12] Schmidt, F., & Hunter, J. (1998). The validity and utility of selection methods in personnel psychology: Practical and theoretical implications of 85 years of research findings. *Psychological Bulletin, 124*(2), 262–274.

[13] Hardy, J. H., Ness, A. M., & Mecca, J. (2017). Outside the box: Epistemic curiosity as a predictor of creative problem solving and creative performance. *Personality and Individual Differences, 104*, 230–237.

[14] Acurantes, L. (2016, November 25). Why you should hire curious employees. *Human Resources Director.* Retrieved from https://www.hcamag.com/hr-news/why-you-should-hire-curious-employees-227514.aspx

[15] Meyer, K. (2014, February 6). How to hire curious people and keep curiosity alive. *Forbes.* Retrieved from https://www.forbes.com/sites/85broads/2014/02/06/how-to-hire-curious-people-and-keep-curiosity-alive/#6cb78e0794e3

[16] First Round Review. (n.d.). Hire a top performer every time with these interview questions. Retrieved from http://firstround.com/review/hire-a-top-performer-every-time-with-these-interview-questions/

Chapter 9

[1,2] New Vantage Partners. (2018). *Big data executive survey 2018*. Boston: Author.

[3] Wallace, J. C., Little, L. M., Hill, A. D., & Ridge, J. W. (2010). CEO regulatory foci, environmental dynamism, and small firm performance. *Journal of Small Business Management, 48*(4), 580–604.

[4] Collins, J. (2009). *How the mighty fall: And why some companies never give in.* New York: HarperCollins.

[5] Richardson, M., Abraham, C., & Bond, R. (2012). Psychological correlates of university students' academic performance: A systematic review and meta-analysis. *Psychological Bulletin, 138*(2), 353–387.

[6] Boone, C., De Brabander, B., & Hellemans, J. (2000). Research Note: CEO locus of control and small firm performance. *Organization Studies, 21*(3), 641–646.

[7] Berger, W. (2015, September 11). Why curious people are destined for the C-suite. *Harvard Business Review.* Retrieved from https://hbr.org/2015/09/why-curious-people-are-destined-for-the-c-suite

[8] Collins, J., & Porras, J. (1994). *Built to last: Successful habits of visionary companies.* New York: Harper Business.

[9] Grove, A. (2010). *Only the paranoid survive: How to exploit the crisis points that challenge every company* (p. 89). New York: Random House.

[10] Collins, J. (2001). *Good to great* (p. 20). New York: Harper Business.

Chapter 10

[1,2] Cain, S. (2013). *Quiet: The power of introverts in a world that can't stop talking.* New York: Random House Inc.

[3] Greenfield, P. M. (2012). The changing psychology of culture from 1800 to 2000. *Psychological Science, 24*(9), 1722–1731.

[4] Gansberg, M. (1964, March 27). 37 who saw murder didn't call the police. *The New York Times.* Retrieved from https://www.nytimes.com/1964/03/27/37-who-saw-murder-didnt-call-the-police.html

[5] Merry, S. (2016, June 29). Her shocking murder became the stuff of legend. But everyone got the story wrong. *The Washington Post.* Retrieved from https://www.washingtonpost.com/lifestyle/style/her-shocking-murder-became-the-stuff-of-legend-but-everyone-got-the-story-wrong/2016/06/29/544916d8-3952-11e6-9ccd-d6005beac8b3_story.html?utm_term=.5c913f83b59f

[6] Amato, P. R. (1983). Helping behavior in urban and rural environments: Field studies based on a taxonomic organization of helping episodes. *Journal of Personality and Social Psychology, 45*(3), 571–586.

[7] Steblay, N. M. (1987). Helping behavior in rural and urban environments: A meta-analysis. *Psychological Bulletin, 102*(3), 346–356.

[8] Konrath, S. H., O'Brien, E. H., & Hsing, C. (2011). Changes in dispositional empathy in American college students over time: A meta-analysis. *Personality and Social Psychology Review, 15*(2), 180–198.

[9] Turkle, S. (2015, September 27). Stop Googling. Let's talk. *The New York Times.* Retrieved from http://www.nytimes.com/2015/09/27/opinion/sunday/stop-googling-lets-talk.html?_r=0

[10] Berdik, C. (2014). A different abstinence education. *Slate.* Retrieved from http://www.slate.com/articles/technology/future_tense/2015/06/disconnect_project_teenagers_give_up_smartphones_for_a_week.html

[11] Cigna. (2018, May 1). *New Cigna study reveals loneliness at epidemic levels in America.* [Press release]. Retrieved from https://www.cigna.com/newsroom/news-releases/2018/pdf/new-cigna-study-reveals-loneliness-at-epidemic-levels-in-america.pdf

[12] Holt-Lunstand, J., Smith, T. B., & Layton, J. B. (2010). Social relationships and mortality risk: A meta-analytic review. *PLOS Medicine, 7*(7). Retrieved from http://journals.plos.org/plosmedicine/article?id=10.1371/journal.pmed.1000316

Chapter 11

[1] Turkle, S. (2015, September 27). Stop Googling. Let's talk. *The New York Times.* Retrieved from https://www.nytimes.com/2015/09/27/opinion/sunday/stop-googling-lets-talk.html?_r=0

[2] Turkle, S. (2012, April 21). The flight from conversation. *The New York Times.* Retrieved from https://www.nytimes.com/2012/04/22/opinion/sunday/the-flight-from-conversation.html

[3] Uhls, Y. T., Michikyan, M., Morris, J., Garcia, D., Small, G. W., Zgourou, E., & Greenfield, P. M. (2014). Five days at outdoor education camp without screens improves preteen skills with nonverbal emotion cues. *Computers in Human Behavior, 39*(October), 387–392.

[4] Barnwell, P. (2014, April 22). My students don't know how to have a conversation. *The Atlantic.* Retrieved from https://www.theatlantic.com/education/archive/2014/04/my-students-dont-know-how-to-have-a-conversation/360993/

[5] Baker, D. A., & Algorta, G. P. (2016). The relationship between online social networking and depression: A systematic review of quantitative studies. *Cyberpsychology, Behavior, and Social Networking, 19*(11), 638–648.

[6] Olds, J., & Schwartz, R. (2009). *The lonely American: Drifting apart in the 21ˢᵗ century.* Boston: Beacon Press.

[7] Marcus, M. B. (2016, October 12). Feeling lonely? So are a lot of other people, survey finds. *CBSNews.com.* Retrieved from http://www.cbsnews.com/news/many-americans-are-lonely-survey-finds/

[8] Anwar, Y. (2015, February 12). Creating love in the lab: The 36 questions that spark intimacy. *Berkeley News*. Retrieved from http://news.berkeley.edu/2015/02/12/love-in-the-lab/

[9] Aron, E. (2015, March 18). 36 questions for intimacy, back story. *Huffington Post*. Retrieved from https://www.huffingtonpost.com/elaine-aron-phd/36-questions-for-intimacy_b_6472282.html

[10] Catron, M. L. (2015, January 11). To fall in love with anyone, do this. *The New York Times*. Retrieved from https://www.nytimes.com/2015/01/11/fashion/modern-love-to-fall-in-love-with-anyone-do-this.html

[11] Aron, A., Melinat, E., Aron, E., Vallone, R. D., & Bastor, R. J. (1997). The experimental generation of interpersonal closeness: A procedure and some preliminary findings. *Personality and Social Psychology Bulletin, 23*(4), 363–377.

[12] Acevedo, B., & Aron, A. (2014). Romantic love, pair-bonding, and the dopaminergic reward system. In M. Mikulincer & P. R. Shaver (Eds.), *Mechanisms of social connection: From brain to group* (pp. 55–70). Washington, DC: American Psychological Association.

Chapter 12

[1] Kashdan, T. B., & Roberts, J. (2004). Trait and state curiosity in the genesis of intimacy: Differentiation from related constructs. *Journal of Social and Clinical Psychology, 23*(6), 792–816.

[2] Kashdan, T. B., McKnight, P. E., Fincham, F. D., & Rose, P. (2011). When curiosity breeds intimacy: Taking advantage of intimacy opportunities and transforming boring conversations. *Journal of Personality, 79*(6), 1369–1401.

[3, 5, 6] Singer, T., & Klimecki, O. M. (2014). Empathy and compassion. *Current Biology, 24*(18), R875–R878.

[4] Neumann, M., Edelhäuser, F., Tauschel, D., Fischer, M. R., Wirtz, M., et al. (2011). Empathy decline and its reasons: A systematic review of studies with medical students and residents. *Academic Medicine, 86*(8), 996–1009.

[7] Batson, C. D. (2009). These things called empathy: Eight related but distinct phenomena. In J. Decety & W. Ickes (Eds.), *The social neuroscience of empathy* (pp. 3–15). Cambridge, MA: MIT Press.

[8] Fredericksen, B. L., Cohn, M. A., Coffey, K. A., Pek, J., & Finkel, S. M. (2008). Open hearts build lives: Positive emotions, induced through loving-kindness meditation, build consequential resources. *Journal of Personal Social Psychology, 95,* 1045–1062.

[9] Covey, S. (1989) *The 7 habits of highly effective people: Powerful lessons in personal change*. New York: Simon & Schuster.

[10] Ehrenreich, B. (1985, February 21). Hers. *The New York Times*. Retrieved from http://www.nytimes.com/1985/02/21/garden/hers.html

Chapter 13

[1, 7] Sherman, E. (2015, September 30). America is the richest, and most unequal, country. *Forbes*. Retrieved from http://fortune.com/2015/09/30/america-wealth-inequality/

[2] U.S. Census Bureau, Table P-1. Total CPS population and per capita income. Retrieved from www.census.gov/data/tables/time-series/demo/income-poverty/historical-income-people.html

[3] Sachs, J. (2017). Restoring American happiness. In J. Helliwell, R. Layard, & J. Sachs (Eds.), *World Happiness Report*. New York: Sustainable Development Solutions Network.

[4] Gallup Organization. (2017). *Gallup 2017 Global Emotions*. New York: Author.

[5] Glaser, G. (2017, December 29). America, can we talk about your drinking? *The New York Times*, p. SR4.

[6] Centers for Disease Control. (2018). *Prescription opioid overdose data*. Retrieved from https://www.cdc.gov/drugoverdose/data/overdose.html

[8, 9, 11] Diener, E., & Biswas-Diener, R. (2002). Will money increase subjective well-being? *Social Indicators Research, 57*(2), 119–169.

[10] Kahneman, D., & Deaton, A. (2010). High income improves evaluation of life but not emotional well-being. *Proceedings of the National Academies of Sciences, 107*(38), 16489–16493.

[12, 14] Ryan, R. M., & Deci, E. (2001). On happiness and human potentials: A review of research on hedonic and eudaimonic well-being. *Annual Review of Psychology, 52*, 141–166.

[13] McMahan, E. A., & Estes, D. (2011). Hedonic versus eudaimonic conceptions of well-being: Evidence of differential associations with self-reported well-being. *Social Indicators Research, 103*(1), 93–108.

[15] Peterson, C., Ruch, W., Beermann, U., Park, N., & Seligman, M. E. P. (2007). Strengths of character, orientations to happiness, and life satisfaction. *The Journal of Positive Psychology, 2*(3), 149–156.

[16] Hsee, C., Ruan, B., & Lu, Z. Y. (2015). Creating happiness by first inducing and then satisfying a desire: The case of curiosity. In K. Diehl & C. Yoon (Eds.), *Advances in Consumer Research, 43* (287–291). Duluth, MN: Association for Consumer Research.

[17] Hsee, C., & Ruan, B. (2015). Curiosity kills the cat. In K. Diehl & C. Yoon (Eds.), *Advances in Consumer Research, 43*, (63–64). Duluth, MN: Association for Consumer Research.

[18] Hsee, C. K., & Ruan, B. (2016). The Pandora effect: The power and peril of curiosity. *Psychological Science, 27*(5), 659–666.

Chapter 14

[1] Steger, M. (2010, June 3). The good from the bad: The full life is a blend of the good and the bad. *Psychology Today* [blog post]. Retrieved from https://www.psychologytoday.com/us/blog/the-meaning-in-life/201006/the-good-the-bad

[2, 3] Kashdan, L., & Steger, M. (2007). Curiosity and pathways to well-being and meaning in life: Traits, states, and everyday behaviors. *Motivation and Emotion, 31*(3), 159–173.

[4] Garrosa, E., Blanco-Donoso, L. M., Carmona-Cobo, I., & Moreno-Jimenez, B. (2016). How do curiosity, meaning in life, and search for meaning predict college students' daily emotional exhaustion and engagement? *Journal of Happiness Studies, 18*(1), 1–24.

[5, 6] Peterson, C., Ruch, W., Beermann, U., Park, N., & Seligman, M. E. P. (2007). Strengths of character, orientations to happiness, and life satisfaction. *The Journal of Positive Psychology, 2*(3), 149–156.

[7, 8] Kaczmarek, L., Baczkowski, B., Enko, J., Baran, B., & Theuns, P. (2014). Subjective well-being as a mediator for curiosity and depression. *Polish Psychological Bulletin, 45*(2), 200–204.

[9] Stone, A. A., Schwartz, J. E., Broderick, J. E., & Deaton, A. (2010) A snapshot of the age distribution of psychological well-being in the United States. *Proceedings of the National Academies of Science, 107*(22), 9985–9990.

[10, 11] Chisholm, D. (2016, December 2). After the midlife crisis: Why your happy years start at 50. *Noted.* Retrieved from https://www.noted.co.nz/health/psychology/after-the-midlife-crisis-why-your-happy-years-start-at-50/

[12] Robinson, O., Demetre, J. D., & Litman, J. A. (2016). Adult life stage and crisis as predictors of curiosity and authenticity: Testing inferences from Erikson's lifespan theory. *International Journal of Behavioral Development, 41*(3), 1–6.

Chapter 15

[1] Phillips, R., Evans, B., & Muirhead, S. (2015). Curiosity, place, and well-being: Encouraging place-specific curiosity as a "way to well-being." *Environment and Planning, 47*(11), 2339–2354.

[2] Whippman, R. (2016). *America the anxious: How our pursuit of happiness is creating a nation of nervous wrecks.* New York: St. Martin's Press.

[3] Mauss, I. B., Savino, N. S., Anderson, C. L., Weisbuch, M., Tamir, M., & Laudenslager, M. L. (2011). The pursuit of happiness can be lonely. *Emotion, 12*(5), 908–912.

[4] Whippman, R. (2016, December 22). America is obsessed with happiness—and it's making us miserable. *Vox.* Retrieved from https://www.vox.com/first-person/2016/10/4/13093380/happiness-america-ruth-whippman

[5] Whippman, R. (2017, October 27). Happiness is other people. *The New York Times*. Retrieved from https://www.nytimes.com/2017/10/27/opinion/sunday/happiness-is-other-people.html

[6] NPD Group. (2014, August 6). *Consumers are alone over half of eating occasions as a result of changing lifestyles and more single-person households, reports NPD.* [Press release]. Retrieved from https://www.npd.com/wps/portal/npd/us/news/press-releases/consumers-are-alone-over-half-of-eating-occasions-as-a-result-of-changing-lifestyles-and-more-single-person-households-reports-npd/; Twenge, J. M. (2017, September 2017). Have smartphones destroyed a generation? *The Atlantic*. Retrieved from https://www.theatlantic.com/magazine/archive/2017/09/has-the-smartphone-destroyed-a-generation/534198/

[7] Ryan, R. M., & Deci, E. (2001). On happiness and human potentials: A review of research on hedonic and eudaimonic well-being. *Annual Review of Psychology, 52,* 141–166.

[8] Gallup Organization. (2017). *Gallup 2017 Global Emotions.* New York: Author.

[9] Demir, M., Özdemir, M., & Weitekamp, L. A. (2007). Looking to happy tomorrows with friends: Best and close friendships as they predict happiness. *Journal of Happiness Studies, 8,* 243–271.

[10, 11] Malcolm, L. (2013). Does curiosity trump happiness in the wellbeing stakes? *Australian Broadcasting Corporation.* Retrieved from http://www.abc.net.au/radionational/programs/allinthemind/curiosity/4692056

Chapter 16

[1] Tavernise, S., & Seelye, K. Q. (2016, November 15). Political divide splits relationships—and Thanksgiving, too. *The New York Times*. Retrieved from https://www.nytimes.com/2016/11/16/us/political-divide-splits-relationships-and-thanksgiving-too.html

[2] Pew Research Center. (2017, October 5). *The partisan divide on political values grows even wider.* Retrieved from http://www.people-press.org/2017/10/05/the-partisan-divide-on-political-values-grows-even-wider/

[3, 4] Iyengar, S., & Westwood, S. J. (2014). Fear and loathing across party lines: New evidence on group polarization. *American Journal of Political Science, 59*(3), 690–707.

[5] Silverman, C. (2016, November 16). This analysis shows how viral fake election news stories outperformed real news on Facebook. *BuzzFeed News*. Retrieved from https://www.buzzfeed.com/craigsilverman/viral-fake-election-news-outperformed-real-news-on-facebook?utm_term=.ldB9EY368#.eeO0yOGMw

[6] Herrman, J. (2016, August 24). Inside Facebook's (totally insane, unintentionally gigantic, hyperpartisan) political-media machine: How a strange new class of media outlet has arisen to take over our news feeds. *The New York Times*

Magazine. Retrieved from https://www.nytimes.com/2016/08/28/magazine/inside-facebooks-totally-insane-unintentionally-gigantic-hyperpartisan-political-media-machine.html

[7] Smith, A., & Banic, V. (2016, December 9). Fake news: How a partying Macedonian teen earns thousands publishing lies. *NBC News.* Retrieved from http://www.nbcnews.com/news/world/fake-news-how-partying-macedonian-teen-earns-thousands-publishing-lies-n692451

[8] Vosoughi, S., Roy, D., & Aral, S. (2018). The spread of true and false news online. *Science, 359*(6380), 1146–1151.

[9] Kahneman, D. (2011). *Thinking fast and slow.* New York: Farrar, Straus & Giroux.

[10] Cohen, G. (2003). Party over policy: The dominating impact of group influence on political beliefs. *Journal of Personality and Social Psychology, 85*(5), 808–822.

[11] Arum, R., & Roksa, J. (2011). *Academically adrift: Limited learning on college campuses.* Chicago: University of Chicago Press.

[12] Belkin, D. (2015, January 16). Test finds college graduates lack skills for white-collar jobs. *The Wall Street Journal.* Retrieved from http://www.wsj.com/articles/test-finds-many-students-ill-prepared-to-enter-workforce-1421432744

[13] Haidt, J. (2006). *The happines hypothesis: Finding modern truth in ancient wisdom.* New York: Basic Books.

[14, 16] Kahan, D., Landrum, A., Carpenter, K., Helft, L., & Jamieson, K. H. (2017). Science curiosity and political information processing. *Advances in Political Psychology, 38*(S1), 179–199.

[15] Nyhan, B., Reifler, J., Richey, S., & Freed, G. L. (2014). Effective messages in vaccine promotion: A randomized trial. *Pediatrics, 133*(4), 2013–2365.

[17] Frimer, J. A., Skitka, L. J., & Motyl, M. (2017). Liberals and conservatives are similarly motivated to avoid exposure to one another's opinions. *Journal of Experimental Social Psychology, 72,* 1–12.

[18] Frimer, J. A., Skitka, L. J., & Motyl, M. (2017, January 4). Liberals and conservatives have one thing in common: Zero interest in opposing views. *Los Angeles Times.* Retrieved from http://www.latimes.com/opinion/op-ed/la-oe-frimer-skitka-motyle-motivated-ignorance-20170104-story.html

Chapter 17

[1] Tocqueville, A. (1898). *Democracy in America, Vol. 1.* Translated by Henry Reeve. New York: The Century Company.

[2] Lührmann, A., Lindberg, S. I., Mechkova, V., Olin, M., Casagrande, F. B., Petrarca, C. S., & Saxer, L. (2017). *Democracy at dusk? V-Dem annual report 2017.* Gothenberg, Germany: University of Gothenberg.

[3] Filipov, D. (2017, March 23). Here are 10 critics of Vladimir Putin who died violently or in suspicious ways. *The Washington Post*. Retrieved from https://www.washingtonpost.com/news/worldviews/wp/2017/03/23/here-are-ten-critics-of-vladimir-putin-who-died-violently-or-in-suspicious-ways/

[4] Mounk, Y., & Foa, R. S. (2016, December 8). Yes, people really are turning away from democracy. *The Washington Post*. Retrieved from https://www.washingtonpost.com/news/wonk/wp/2016/12/08/yes-millennials-really-are-surprisingly-approving-of-dictators/?utm_term=.6d730cd04dc2

Chapter 18

[1] Kahan, D., Landrum, A., Carpenter, K., Helft, L., & Jamieson, K. H. (2017). Science curiosity and political information processing. *Advances in Political Psychology*, *38*(S1), 179–199.

[2] Yang, D. J., Preston, J. L., & Hernandez, I. (2012). Polarized attitudes toward the Ground Zero mosque are reduced by high-level construal. *Social Psychological and Personality Science*, *4*(2), 244–250.

[3] Pew Research Center. (2017, October 5). *The partisan divide on political values grows even wider*. Retrieved from http://www.people-press.org/2017/10/05/the-partisan-divide-on-political-values-grows-even-wider/

[4] Pew Research Center. (2006, March 15). A day in the life of the media. *Project for Excellence in Journalism*. Retrieved from http://stateofthemedia.org/2006/a-day-in-the-life-of-the-media-intro/newspaper/

[5] Brooks, D. (2014, October 27). Why partyism is wrong. *The New York Times*. Retrieved from https://www.nytimes.com/2014/10/28/opinion/david-brooks-why-partyism-is-wrong.html

[6] Brooks, D. (2017, August 22). What moderates believe. *The New York Times*. Retrieved from https://www.nytimes.com/2017/08/22/opinion/trump-moderates-bipartisanship-truth.html

[7] Golden, E. (2017, November 4). 'Reds' and 'blues' sit down together to try to heal the political divide. *Minneapolis Star-Tribune*. Retrieved from http://www.startribune.com/healing-the-political-divide-with-plenty-of-ground-rules/455244103/

[8] Sahlberg, P. (2011). *Finnish lessons: What can the world learn from educational change in Finland?* New York: Teachers' College Press.

Epilogue

[1] Davidson, P. (2017, April 17). Why China is beating the U.S. at innovation. *USA Today*. Retrieved from https://www.usatoday.com/story/money/2017/04/17/why-china-beating-us-innovation/100016138/

Index

About the Author

Bryan Goodwin is president and CEO of McREL International. For 20 years at McREL, he has translated research into practice, scanning the world for new insights and best practices on teaching and leading, and helping educators everywhere adapt them to address their own challenges. A frequent conference presenter, he is the author of *Simply Better: Doing What Matters Most to Change the Odds for Student Success* and coauthor of *Curiosity Works: A Guidebook for Moving Your School from Improvement to Innovation*, *Unstuck: How Curiosity, Peer Coaching, and Teaming Can Change Your School*, *Balanced Leadership for Powerful Learning: Tools for Achieving Success in Your School*, and *The 12 Touchstones of Good Teaching: A Checklist for Staying Focused Every Day*. He also writes for ASCD's *Educational Leadership* magazine. Before joining McREL in 1998, Goodwin was a college instructor, a high school teacher, and a business journalist.

Curiosity, McREL, and your community

Curious about how to increase curiosity in your local schools or organization? Consider collaborating with McREL to activate the power of curiosity in teachers, students, and leaders.

For more than 50 years, McREL's education research and development has produced valuable resources for educators such as Balanced Leadership® and Classroom Instruction That Works®, bringing inspiration and world-class strategies for instruction and leadership to schools of all sizes and contexts. Now we're tying our extensive knowledge base together and embedding it with curiosity-focused training, coaching, and consulting.

Contact us today to learn how our Curiosity Works™ initiative can spark engagement, improvement, and innovation across your school, your district, or your organization.